The Two Lives of
Sally Miller

The Two Lives of Sally Miller

A Case of Mistaken Racial Identity in Antebellum New Orleans

⚊╪

Carol Wilson

Rutgers University Press
New Brunswick, New Jersey, and London

Library of Congress Cataloging-in-Publication Data

Wilson, Carol, 1962–
    The two lives of Sally Miller: A case of mistaken racial identity in antebellum
New Orleans / Carol Wilson.
p.   cm.
    Includes bibliographical references and index.
    ISBN-13: 978–0–8135–4057–3 (hardcover : alk. paper)
    ISBN-13: 978–0–8135–4058–0 (pbk. : alk. paper)
    1. Müller, Salomé, b. ca. 1809. 2. Müller, Salomé, b. ca. 1809—Trials,
litigation, etc. 3. Slaves—Louisiana—New Orleans—Biography. 4. Women,
White—Louisiana—New Orleans—Biography. 5. German Americans—
Louisiana—New Orleans—Biography. 6. Mistaken identity—Louisiana—New
Orleans—Case studies. 7. Trials—Louisiana—New Orleans. 8. Slaves—
Emancipation—Louisiana—New Orleans. 9. New Orleans (La.)—Race relations.
10. New Orleans (La.)—Biography. I. Title.
    F379.N553M559 2007
    305.8009763'35—dc22

                                                            2006027317

A British Cataloging-in-Publication record for this book is available from the British
Library.

Manufactured in the United States of America

To Kevin

CONTENTS

ILLUSTRATIONS

ACKNOWLEDGMENTS

I would like to thank my friends and colleagues for their help with and interest in this project over the years, especially Pam Pears, Wendy Miller, Emilie Amt, Peter Wakefield, Cindy Licata, Albin Kowalewski, and Robert L. Zangrando. I am grateful for the assistance I received in researching the book in New Orleans, particularly from Marie Windell, Connie Mui, and Dennis Kehoe. My editor, Kendra Boileau, and the anonymous readers of Rutgers University Press were extremely skillful in helping me to improve the quality of the manuscript. My father, Calvin D. Wilson, assisted in many ways. Most of all, I would like to thank my husband, Kevin McKillop, for his love and support.

The Two Lives of
Sally Miller

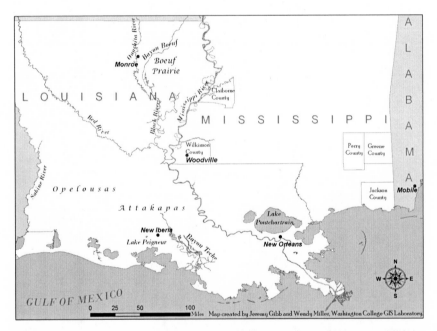

FIGURE 1. Map of Lower Mississippi River Valley, based on 1812 map, publisher unknown, by Jeremy Gibb and Wendy Miller of the Washington College GIS Laboratory.

The Discovery of Salomé Muller

⚍╪

One day in the spring of 1843, Mrs. Karl Rouff, a German immigrant, entered a café on Levée Street in New Orleans. The slave who served her looked familiar; and eventually Madame Karl, as she was known, realized with a shock that she recognized the woman. Madame Karl had last seen her more than two decades earlier when both had arrived in the city with several hundred other Germans. At that time, this woman had been a small child called Salomé Muller. Salomé's mother and infant brother had not survived the voyage from Europe, and her father and older brother had died soon after arriving in Louisiana. Salomé and her sister Dorothea, both under the age of six, had disappeared and had never been seen or heard from since.[1]

Madame Karl questioned the slave, who neither recognized her customer nor recalled emigrating to the United States in 1818. She explained that she was called Sally Miller and was the property of Louis Belmonti, owner of the café. Madame Karl took Sally to the home of Eve and Francis Schuber in the nearby suburb of Lafayette. The Schubers were also German immigrants and had traveled on the same voyage with Madame Karl and the Muller family. In fact, Eve Schuber was Salomé Muller's cousin and godmother.[2] Schuber recalled watching the stranger come up the steps and was struck by her resemblance to the missing child and her family. She asked Madame Karl, "Is that a German woman? I know her."

Madame Karl replied, "If you know her, who is she?"

Schuber answered, "One of the lost Millers." (Schuber here used the anglicized Miller for Muller.) Schuber stated that the family resemblance was strong; beyond that, she recollected Salomé Muller well enough to be able to recognize her "among one hundred thousand persons." Her husband, upon seeing the woman at his house, asked his wife, "Is that one of the girls that were lost?"[3]

Eve Schuber's identification was especially significant: as the niece of Salomé's mother (also named Dorothea), she had been in the constant company of the Muller family on board ship. After Dorothea Muller died on the journey, fifteen-year-old Eve (née Kropp) took over the nursing of little Salomé. Her commitment to the girl's care was such that when they landed in New Orleans, Eve asked her uncle Daniel Muller to allow her to keep Salomé and raise her. Like the other members of her family, however, the little girl was indentured to an Attakapas farmer.[4] Eve herself was also bound out, and it seems unlikely that her master would have permitted her to take responsibility for the care of a young child. Since that time, Eve had served out her indenture in the city and married fellow immigrant Francis Schuber, who had set up business as a butcher. She and her husband had remained in New Orleans, residing first in the Faubourg St. Mary and later moving to the adjacent town of Lafayette.[5] (A faubourg was a suburb or, in French, "false city.") She frequently saw other Germans who had arrived on the same ship; and though she had inquired among them about the Mullers, she had never learned anything about the fate of the missing girls. Eve Schuber did not see Salomé Muller again until the day in 1843 when Madame Karl came to her house with the slave Sally.[6]

With the support of the Schubers, Sally initiated a lawsuit in New Orleans District Court against her owner Louis Belmonti, with her previous, longtime owner John F. Miller called as warrantor.[7] Her petition, filed on January 24, 1844, was nothing short of extraordinary: she declared that she was a free white woman and had been held in slavery illegally for more than two decades. Sally claimed that she had been born of Bavarian parents who had emigrated around 1817. Upon arrival, she, her father, and her three siblings were "sold or bound as Redemptioners to one John Miller who took them into the Parish of Attakapas, and that her father died before he arrived at their place of destination. All of which facts your petitioner has, among other things, since learned, she being of too early an age to have them deeply impressed upon her memory." The petition gave her age as no older than three at the time of the events described.[8]

Sally stated that not only had Miller converted her into a slave, knowing that she was free, but that her present owner, Louis Belmonti, also knew, it "being then a matter of common notoriety" that she had been illegally enslaved. Since she had begun asserting her freedom, she said, Belmonti had "adopted a cruel system of persecution against her," variously threatening to imprison her, put her to work on a chain gang, and sell her at public auction. She feared he intended to kidnap her and so asked the Court for protection under a writ of sequestration, a practice designed to remove property from the party in possession of it during a dispute. She then found herself imprisoned in the Calaboso (the city jail) for a week before being released into Francis Schuber's custody on one thousand dollars bond. In jail she was thrown in with felons and debtors as well as slaves charged with petty crimes for which whites would simply have been fined. Her time could not have been pleasant: the Calaboso was filled to overflowing, and sanitation was rudimentary at best. Illness and escapes were common, as were riots.[9]

Sally's owner, Louis Belmonti, filed his response to her charges on February 2. His statement was simple: the "woman calling herself Sally Miller" was "a slave pretending to be free." Her real name, said Belmonti, was Mary, she had always lived as a slave, and he had purchased her legally from her then-owner, John Miller. He offered in evidence a copy of the bill of sale, notarized on July 9, 1838, showing that Miller had sold Mary to Belmonti for seven hundred dollars. Belmonti added that he had already sustained two hundred dollars' worth of damages from the suit and as a result called Miller into the lawsuit as warrantor.[10] Sally had requested one thousand dollars compensation for the service she had given to Belmonti as his slave; thus, he hoped that, if the suit went against him, Miller would be forced to pay any damages awarded to her. Belmonti also asked that Miller repay Sally's purchase price with interest and cover losses of two hundred dollars—presumably Belmonti's legal fees and possibly the cost of hiring someone to do Sally's work.[11]

After being called into the suit in warranty, John F. Miller became, in effect, the principal defendant since the plaintiff charged that it was he who had enslaved her initially, after purchasing her time as a redemptioner. Miller's lawyers asked the Court to require Sally to produce the redemption contract under which her family had been bound to Miller's service. If she were unable to prove this part of her claim, Miller asked that her suit be dismissed. When the Court failed to grant his request, he began producing documents of his own. He provided three bills of sale for his former slave. One showed her coming into his possession on August 13, 1822, when Anthony Williams of Mobile left Bridget, as she was then known, with Miller. Miller was to sell her for Williams and accepted a one-hundred-dollar advance on the sale. A second document indicated that on February 1, 1823, Miller sold Bridget to his mother, Mrs. Sarah Canby, for 350 dollars. The third bill, dated February 17, 1835, showed Miller buying back Bridget, who by then had three children. All four were sold to him for 350 dollars.[12]

Miller's deposition, filed on April 27, reiterated his legal claim over Bridget and denied the allegations that she was actually a white woman. He had never contracted with any redemptioners, and he always believed his slave to be a mulatto of African descent. Since the sale of Sally to Belmonti in 1838, Miller added, he had become insolvent; in fact, his creditors were in the process of suing him in the same District Court. Even if any liability did exist, which Miller again denied, he asked to be released from the warranty. His request was not granted, and he was still the warrantor when the trial began on May 23, 1844.[13]

The *Miller v. Belmonti* trial held all the elements of a great courtroom drama: a case of mistaken identity, illegal enslavement, the epic journey of an impoverished immigrant family, and the inscrutable past of a young woman whose appearance made her racial categorization difficult. A slave was publicly defying her owner, accusing him of one of the worst crimes an honorable southern gentleman could commit—that of knowingly holding a white woman in bondage. Public reaction to the trial was divided. New Orleans's German community stood by the plaintiff Sally Miller, convinced that she was the lost child they remembered, a victim of tragic circumstances and deliberate abuse. Other New Orleans whites, including some of the city's most prominent citizens, sided with Sally's owner, John Miller, defending his character and affirming her slave status. To them, she embodied the mulatto's worst traits—the black's willingness to lie and cheat and the white's cunning to do so successfully.

As the case, or rather series of cases (five lawsuits in all) unfolded, observers were forced to confront a variety of issues, including race, gender, ethnicity, and class. First and foremost was the question of racial identity. Southern slave owning was predicated on race: blacks were slaves; whites were free. But people of mixed racial background existed, nowhere more noticeably than in Louisiana. And their very existence threatened a system that demanded that race be easily distinguished. That a slave could even claim white status and have that claim considered in court was a possibility that struck terror into the hearts of southern whites. That the slave in this case was a woman merely heightened the emotional response to the crime. Illegally enslaving a white person was wrong, but women, perceived as especially vulnerable in Victorian America, deserved special protection. According to the prevalent Cult of True Womanhood, women embodied four core values: piety, purity, domesticity, and submissiveness. Abolitionists had already made the argument that slavery robbed black women of their virtue. Particularly in

New Orleans, where light-skinned slaves were advertised openly as sexual partners—"fancy girls"—the enslavement of a white woman conjured up particularly disturbing images.

Just as women were vulnerable, so, too, were immigrants, especially those of modest means. As the trial progressed, the Germans who had emigrated with the Muller family told a tale of unimaginable exploitation and abuse. While technically protected from actual enslavement by their race, they had lost their freedom, albeit temporarily, and were forced to labor for strangers. For some immigrants, especially children—in this case, two orphaned sisters—virtual slavery might have turned into actual slavery. Thus, as vulnerable victims of the powerful, wealthy, male elite, the lives of Salomé Muller the immigrant and Sally Miller the slave may not have been so very far apart. The question the trial was to answer was whether they were in fact the same single life.

When Sally Miller the slave claimed to be Salomé Muller the German immigrant, the murky waters of southern racial designation came under scrutiny. From the spectators in the New Orleans courtroom to newspaper readers in the distant North, observers of the case chose sides, all finding information to bolster their different positions. Each witness and each new piece of evidence pulled public opinion first in one direction, then in the other. Two stories were told in the courtroom: the tale of Salomé Muller, a little girl traveling to the New World with her family, and that of Sally, a lifelong slave of African descent. Whether they represented the stories of two different women or one and the same was a question that threatened both the Louisiana legal system and white southerners' notions of race.

CHAPTER 1

A Slave Sues Her Master

⟨≈⟩

*T*he case of *Miller v. Belmonti* went to trial on May 23, 1844, in New Orleans District Court. New Orleans courts, including the First District's, were located in the Presbytère. Although the structure was built during Spanish rule (1767–1800) to house Catholic church leaders, it apparently never served that purpose but was rented out by the church until becoming the court chambers in 1813. Located on one side of St. Louis Cathedral, with the Cabildo (city hall) on the other, the Presbytère formed part of the complex of public buildings facing the Place d'Armes. They appeared grand from the outside but were considerably less so on the inside. An 1847 visitor to the city described the Court's unprepossessing interior, writing that "Applewomen take possession of its lobbies. Beggars besiege its vault like offices. The rains from heaven sport among its rafters. It has everywhere a fatty, ancient smell, which speaks disparagingly of the odor in which justice is held."[1]

Sally's legal team was headed by Wheelock S. Upton. Upton had co-authored *The Civil Code of the State of Louisiana*, published in 1838 by Emile Johns (who ironically later served as a defense witness for John F. Miller). Beyond that fact, little is known about Upton or his brother Frank, who also worked on the case. While Upton was the voice of the prosecution, a more prominent attorney also helped represent Sally. Christian Roselius, a German immigrant, had been born near Bremen in 1803. According to some sources, he came to America as a redemptioner, but others have questioned this claim. Certainly he was not wealthy when he arrived in New Orleans at the age of seventeen. Starting his career as a printer's apprentice, he began reading law and passed the bar in 1828. When the *Miller v. Belmonti* trial began, he had just finished a term as the state's attorney general. He later became a delegate to the constitutional conventions of 1845 and 1852. Perhaps Upton realized after taking on the case that its notoriety would put him in the public eye. He may have felt the need for some strong support against his opponent, one of the best-known lawyers in the state.[2]

FIGURE 2. View of the Place d'Armes, by X. Marigny after Gaston de Pontalba, ca. 1849. *Collection of the Louisiana State Museum.*

About Upton's opponent, John Grymes, much has been written. Born in Virginia in 1786, he came to New Orleans in 1808 and soon "became one of the city's most colorful figures," according to author Robert Tallant. Appointed U.S. District Attorney, he resigned to defend the notorious Lafitte brothers against charges of smuggling. As a result, Grymes was accused in court by the new prosecutor of exchanging his honor for "bloodstained pirate gold." Grymes challenged the man to a duel and crippled him for life. (This was not the only duel he fought; Grymes also attacked a fellow legislator during a session of the state legislature.) He aided Andrew Jackson in his battle against the U.S. Bank and represented the litigious illegitimate heiress Myra Clark Gaines (see the conclusion of this book). His high earnings supported a lavish lifestyle; he was known for elaborate dinners given for visiting dignitaries, including the Duke of Saxe-Weimar-Eisenach and Henry Clay.[3]

The plaintiff's witnesses testified first. There were eleven in all, seven of them German immigrants who had journeyed to this country with the Mullers in 1818. All remembered the little girl, Salomé Muller, and either noted the plaintiff's strong resemblance to members of the Muller family or recognized her more specifically as the missing girl. Sally herself did not

FIGURE 3. John Randolph Grymes, by Theodore F. Moise. 1842. *Courtesy of the Historic New Orleans Collection, accession no. 1959–83.*

testify.[4] As a slave initiating a legal action, her situation was unusual. Other slave states required slaves to have a court-appointed guardian initiate a lawsuit on their behalf. According to historian Judith Kelleher Schafer, "The ability of a slave to sue for freedom directly was unique to Louisiana." This right derived from the Spanish code of law which granted slaves *coartacion*, the ability to purchase their freedom. To make such transactions, slaves were granted standing in court. Although *coartacion* did not survive the transfer to American control, the ability to sue directly for freedom did. This was the only instance in which slaves had legal standing.[5]

Throughout American history, there is little evidence of slaves' physical presence in the courtroom. As Ariela Gross has written, "The central subject of a dispute, graphically brought to life in testimony, embodied in words, may not have actually appeared in person very often in the courtroom."[6] Sally simply lacked the knowledge necessary to make her case. In her petition, she claimed that, until the arrival of Madame Karl and Eve Schuber into her life, she had had no idea of her true past as a German immigrant. Sally had been too young to remember her enslavement and had grown up accepting her status as a slave without question. She now relied on her countrymen and women to tell the story of her life, and this they did with alacrity.

Those giving testimony included three German women who had traveled across the Atlantic with the Mullers. Madame Hemm was from Württemberg and had first met the Mullers at the Dutch port of Den Helder. Mrs. Schultzheimer, now a midwife, had lived on a farm several miles from the Mullers and had grown up with Sally's mother. Mrs. Fleikener was related to Salomé Muller by marriage: her first husband's mother was Daniel Muller's sister. All three testified that the plaintiff was the little girl they remembered from the journey, and all noted the resemblance she bore to the adult Mullers they had known, especially Salomé's mother. Eve Schuber went one step further, saying that she had known Salomé Muller well enough to recognize her in a crowd of a thousand people.[7] Daniel Miller, nephew of Salomé's father, Daniel (the nephew's name had been anglicized), also gave evidence. After arriving in this country in 1818, he and his father and brothers had been taken as redemptioners to Wilkinson County, Mississippi, where they had lived ever since. His family was in the habit of going to New Orleans about once a year to look for their missing cousins but had not heard anything until May 1843, when the Schubers had contacted him. He provided the most direct genetic link to Salomé Muller and stated firmly that he believed the plaintiff was his cousin. The Court record stated, "He has no hesitancy in saying he has no doubt but that she is the same person."[8]

These identifications offered persuasive testimony, but Eve Schuber provided additional evidence. Not only did she claim to recognize the slave as the missing Salomé, but she offered physical proof of her identity. As the child's godmother, Schuber said she had cared for little Salomé after her mother's death on board ship and, as a result, was aware that Sally had two moles on the insides of her thighs. These would provide indisputable proof of her identity. Schuber's husband, Francis, although he had not personally seen the marks, recalled his mother-in-law saying that if Salomé were ever lost, she could be identified "at the end of a hundred years" by certain marks, although he remembered them coming from a burn the child had gotten as an infant. Mrs. Schulzheimer, too, recalled seeing the marks on the infant Sally's legs, shown to her by the girl's mother.[9]

Two physicians examined the plaintiff to verify the existence of the birthmarks. Dr. Armand Mercier and Dr. Warren Stone, one chosen by each side in the case, were prominent New Orleans physicians.[10] Born in New Orleans, Mercier had trained to become a physician in Paris and then returned home and began a distinguished career as a surgeon. Stone may have been the first to use quinine to treat yellow fever and, according to historian of medicine John Duffy, was "probably Louisiana's greatest antebellum surgeon."[11] The two doctors examined Sally and issued a report that described the two marks on her thighs. They agreed that the marks were *navi materi*; in other words, she had been born with them.[12]

Considerable questioning was devoted to both Sally the slave's movements and the movements and residences of the German witnesses. The defense argued that these witnesses surely would have encountered Sally in the city during the past twenty years and recognized her, if she were truly the missing girl. But most of the German witnesses had been indentured soon after coming to New Orleans, many serving their terms outside of the city. Mrs. Schultzheimer, for example, was sent on arrival to the Hopkins plantation; Mrs. Fleikener spent her first eighteen months on Maunsel White's plantation; Madame Hemm spent four years in Baton Rouge. This, the prosecution argued, helped to explain why they had not chanced to see Sally before and why they had been unable to keep track of the dispersal of each member of the Muller family. Eve Kropp lived in the Faubourg Marigny for two years after her arrival while serving out her own indenture. She then married fellow immigrant Francis Schuber, who had established himself as a butcher. For about twenty years, he sold meat in the First Municipality Market on the levée. The Schubers had taken up residence first in the Faubourg St. Mary, later moving to a house along the waterfront in the neighboring suburb of Lafayette. Eve Schuber related that she had frequently encountered other Germans who had come over on the same ship; and though she had asked them about the Mullers, she had never gained any knowledge of the missing girls' whereabouts.[13] By the time of the trial a large German community lived in Lafayette, as did Sally, who had taken up residence there with the Schubers. Lafayette bordered the city proper at Felicity Street, encompassing today's Garden District. Not far in modern terms, it was nonetheless about two miles south from where John Miller and Louis Belmonti and their slave Sally had lived in the Faubourg Marigny. For people who would have gotten about mainly by walking, it was perhaps distance enough to prevent any interaction between residents of different communities, although there was omnibus service to New Orleans by the 1830s. The defense emphasized, however, that German immigrants were also to be found in the Faubourg Marigny, where Sally had lived while she was held as both Miller's and Belmonti's slave.[14]

Most of the prosecution testimony, however, centered on events quite distant in time and space from antebellum New Orleans. In recalling the little girl Salomé Muller, the German witnesses spun an astonishing tale of the hope and tragedy of a group of immigrants struggling to make new lives in a new land. They told a story not just of the life of one little girl but of a family and a community as well. Those attending the trial found themselves transported back to Alsace, some thirty years previously.

CHAPTER 2

The Mullers of Alsace

◄══╬►

$\int$ alomé Muller, known as Sally, was
born in Alsace on July 10, 1813. She was the family's third child; her
brother Jacob had arrived in 1808, her sister Dorothea in 1810. Her mother,
also named Dorothea, had given birth to another son, named Daniel for his
father, in February 1817.[1] The family lived in the village of Langensultzbach
on the Rhine River near the city of Strasbourg. The Mullers and their neighbors were farmers and artisans; Daniel Muller was a lockmaster, his brother
Henry a shoemaker.[2]

Although Alsace had been a French province since 1648, the majority of the population was culturally more German than French. Indeed, people called Germans in the early nineteenth century came from a variety of
states. Historian Marianne Wokeck notes that "German-speaking" is a more
accurate term, especially when referring to those from the western Rhine lands
of Alsace, Lorraine, and Switzerland. Residents of Alsace had been speaking a German dialect, Alemannic, for centuries.[3]

The Mullers left Alsace in April 1817, traveling in a large party that
included relatives and neighbors.[4] This act placed them at the heart of a
historical migration. Beginning late in 1816, in what was known as the
Auswanderung ("wandering out"), thousands of Germans left their homes,
especially in the Rhenish provinces and southwestern states. A little less
than half of these migrants set out for the United States.[5]

Such emigration was by no means a new phenomenon. Indeed, continual movement throughout previous centuries had given people in the region
a reputation for wanderlust. Their reasons for leaving, however, were far from
frivolous. For much of the 1700s, people had been moving to escape problems that Wokeck terms "common to life in pre-industrial societies." The
population of Europe increased by 70 percent between 1720 and 1800.
According to historian Carl Brasseaux, "Growth of the Alsatian population
was particularly explosive." Over time resources proved insufficient to
support the increase.[6]

The states along the Rhine were characterized by a high population density relative to the amount of land, not all of which was well suited to agriculture. The partible system of inheritance, which dictated that lands be divided among all living children, caused plots to shrink in size over time. By 1800 many farms had become too small to support families. Fewer and fewer young people retained access to land, and they had difficulty securing jobs and housing. Fuel sources were becoming scarce; by the nineteenth century, many wooded areas of the southwest (especially the Black Forest) had been stripped nearly bare to provide timber for Europe's expanding navies.[7]

The year 1817, according to economic historian Farley Grubb, "produced the largest single-year spike in German migration to America up to that time." While several factors combined to produce such a phenomenon, one in particular stands out. The suddenness of emigration suggests that some kind of catastrophe occurred in the region, which indeed was the case. Throughout Europe, and in fact much of the world, 1816 was known as the "year without a summer."[8]

Hot weather began early in February, but then temperatures began to fall in April and continued to drop throughout the summer. Rainfall rose until it reached a yearly total six times higher than that of 1814. Dams burst, valleys flooded, farms were inundated, and crops destroyed. The meager harvest began in October, only to be interrupted by the sudden onset of winter. Still, people in agrarian societies are accustomed to good years and bad and can survive the occasional poor harvest. But 1816 was the fourth year of especially cold weather around the world. In the Rhenish provinces the impact of bad weather on crops had already been felt in 1815. The cumulative result was that 1817 saw one of the most severe famines in European history. The important wine industry was badly damaged. Grains became soaked, making bread baking difficult and causing the price of grain and bread to rise considerably, particularly in eastern France. A plague of mice attacked the villages. The very young and very old, always vulnerable, suffered the most and often did not survive.[9]

Other factors exacerbated the weather's deleterious effect on crop production. The Napoleonic wars had cost the people of the Rhine lands a heavy price in the loss of able-bodied men as well as economic disruption caused by wartime taxation. Public funds were seized, the army requisitioned food and clothing for the troops, and even private citizens had their harvests confiscated. Restricted access to communal woodlands, as well as their decreasing productivity, added to fuel expenses. And between 1812 and 1814 military levies in France were expanded, resulting in widespread peasant unrest.[10]

With the economic downturn, artisans such as Daniel and Henry Muller lost customers who could no longer afford their services. About half of all craft workers employed only themselves (and possibly nuclear family members). Weavers, tailors, and shoemakers were still socially and economically better off than wage laborers but were facing more and more competition from cottage industries. At war's end, more competition arrived, in the form of cheap, factory-made goods from Britain. According to historian Stanley Nadel, "It was noted at the time that artisans (who did not grow their own food) were especially vulnerable to famine and were therefore disproportionately numerous among the migrants." [11]

Alsatians were even more directly affected by the fighting. The geographic position of the Rhine lands resulted in repeated invasions and traversings of both the French and Allied armies. The region had been characterized by upheaval for centuries, but the situation had grown urgent in the 1790s with the rise to power of the Jacobins. In what became known as the "Great Flight," between 40,000 and 50,000 Alsatians fled, seeking asylum in German states across the Rhine. Permitted to return several years later, they found that their homes and farms had been confiscated.[12]

A brief lull in the chaos occurred during the period of the Empire, but Allied invasion in 1814 caused the government to close the city of Strasbourg. Invading armies, including nearly 300,000 in the Bas-Rhin (the French administrative term for the northern part of Alsace) alone, introduced a typhus epidemic. The Hundred Days—Napoleon's brief return to rule after the Bourbon restoration—brought another Allied invasion; and by September 1815, more than a million foreign troops occupied French soil. Having already borne the brunt of repeated invasions and requisitioning, the eastern provinces were, according to André Jardin and André-Jean Tudesq, "ruined." When the occupation ended, the frontier cities such as Strasbourg had been supplanted by Mediterranean seaports.[13]

By the time the "year without a summer" struck in 1816, then, many Alsatians were already stressed to the breaking point. Emigration represented the only alternative for a people whose whole world seemed to have turned against them. When American and Russian labor recruiters arrived in the region, spinning "fantastic tales" about opportunities, especially the availability of land, many in the Rhenish provinces left their homes for good. Tens of thousands of Alsatians fled, many not even waiting for their government-issued passports, and the Mullers were among them.[14]

Like others from the European interior, the Muller family faced a long overland journey just to get to the point of embarkation where their sea voyage would begin. Several routes were available. Germans from the south journeyed to Rotterdam and other Netherlands ports, which were accessible to the river network formed by the Rhine and its tributaries, most prominently the Maine, Neckar, and Mosel rivers. This network comprised one of the most-utilized migration routes in the region.[15] When free of ice, rivers provided the easiest means of transport. By contrast, overland travel (usually by mail coach) was at this time arduous, time-consuming, and expensive; however, roads parallel to the Rhine made it possible to move on and off the river as needed. Although he traveled in an earlier era, the Württemburger Gottlieb Mittelberger reported taking seven weeks in 1750 to reach Rotterdam from Heilbron on the Neckar, about the same distance as the Mullers traveled. The slow pace was caused partly by his having to contend with no fewer than thirty-six customs stops on the way. (The *Zollverein*, or customs union, was formed in 1819 to reduce this bureaucratic chaos.) Upon reaching Rotterdam, Mittelberger remained there for some time, commenting that a five- to six-week wait was common.[16]

During the Auswanderung, so many people arrived in such a short time that they clogged the Dutch seaports, and police began turning travelers away at the borders. By early spring, some would-be emigrants were returning home penniless, their funds exhausted by the fruitless journey. In mid-May, the Baden government prohibited further emigration, and in June, Württemberg tightened its restrictions.[17]

By then, however, the Mullers had already arrived in Holland. Daniel's family, Henry's family, Eve Kropp and her future husband Francis Schuber, along with several neighbors had left Alsace in April and made their way up the Rhine toward the port of Amsterdam. They arrived in early August and booked passage to Philadelphia, planning ultimately to settle further inland in the Pennsylvania farm country. Accordingly, they were sent on to Den Helder, the large North Sea port in northern Holland from which large ocean-going vessels departed. Exhausted from their journey, likely homesick and apprehensive about the impending sea voyage, their real problems began while they were awaiting passage at Den Helder.[18]

They expected to travel as part of a group of some nine hundred persons on a huge Russian ship, the *Rudolph*. After they had boarded and loaded their baggage, however, the captain refused to transport them, claiming he had not been paid. A number of the passengers later recalled that the captain had become bankrupt, but in fact the travelers had been robbed.

FIGURE 4. Map of Rhine River area, 1812, based on Gardiner map of 1892, by Jeremy Gibb and Wendy Miller of the Washington College GIS Laboratory.

Immigrant J. C. Wagner reported that the travelers discovered that the men who had "received the passage money in Amsterdam ran away with the money." [19]

This kind of fraud was not an isolated occurrence. Vulnerable and unknowledgeable about the journey they were undertaking, immigrants were easily duped by professional confidence men as well as unscrupulous ships' agents and captains. When government representatives came from Baden, for example, to buy grain for people stranded in Amsterdam, they found multitudes there who claimed that they had been swindled by labor agents. Particular mention was made of a Captain Stein of Strasbourg, who had collected money from people and disappeared. This story was widely broadcast by the government officials across the river at Kahlsruhe, but such warnings were dismissed as scare tactics designed to halt the migration. [20]

And so the Mullers and their compatriots were stranded some four hundred miles from home, on board ship in a North Sea port, with winter approaching and supplies dwindling. There they remained for several months. Conditions on the ship were appalling. Witnesses reported that at least two hundred families occupied the large ship, while others were berthed on smaller ships in the port.[21]

When their supplies were exhausted, the travelers were taken back to Amsterdam where, as Sally's godmother Eve Schuber (then Kropp) recounted, "being poor [they] were obliged to beg." Eventually the Dutch government offered thirty thousand guilders (about twelve thousand dollars) to any captain or merchant who would transport them to the United States. The offer was taken up by a man identified by most of the passengers as Captain Grandsteever, who procured three ships to take the stranded Germans to New Orleans. J. C. Wagner remembered that the captain was paid by the Dutch government and was to take them "for free." They left Amsterdam for the second and final time in December 1817, setting sail not as they had intended for Philadelphia but bound instead for New Orleans.[22]

In the early nineteenth century, the ocean journey from Europe to North America typically took three to four months. Living conditions on board ranged from rudimentary to horrific, causing one historian to term an immigrant ship "a floating hell." [23] Most immigrants traveled in steerage, crammed into the ship's hold with little space, privacy, or facilities for cooking or washing. Only the wealthy could afford to travel in cabins and be treated as passengers in the fullest sense of the word.[24] The rest were literally considered cargo. Ventilation in the hold was virtually nonexistent, creating a particularly gruesome situation given the overcrowding, sickness, and absence of adequate sanitation. Lack of fresh water and food was also a problem. There were no hospital facilities; and because the ill remained among the well, contagious diseases spread rapidly. Thus, many did not survive the voyage.[25]

Until the middle of the nineteenth century, most ships did not furnish passengers with any necessities. Other than fire and water, they were required to bring whatever they needed to survive. The price they paid for passage was not especially high, although the cost of provisioning had to be factored in.[26] German ships, however, often charged higher prices and provided supplies for their travelers. The *Elizabeth*, which sailed from Amsterdam in May 1819, bound for Philadelphia with many German emigrants on board, provides an indication of the charges accumulated on such ships. Passengers signed contracts, agreeing to be "quiet and orderly," to obey the captain, and to pay the following fees: 180 francs for adults (age twelve and older) and 90 francs for children ages four to twelve; children under four traveled for free. Those lacking the required funds could also negotiate partial payment, the balance to be paid within ten days after arrival. Families also had to pay the costs of individuals who died on board, once the journey had progressed beyond the halfway point. In return, the captain agreed to carry the passengers, "accommodate them with the necessary comfort," and give them whatever food rations were stipulated by the contract.[27]

Space limits were not delineated, and overcrowding was a severe problem. The first U.S. law to regulate immigration, passed in 1819, permitted only two passengers per five tons of weight; this included not only cargo but also the weight of the vessel itself and did not count crew members. As a result, travelers often had wholly inadequate living quarters. The construction of ships especially designed for transporting immigrants did not begin until the 1830s; until that time people simply occupied part of the cargo space.[28]

Captains frequently leased space to emigrant agents and assumed no responsibility for the well-being of passengers. According to Friedrich Kapp, chair of the New York Board of Emigration Commissioners, "To the owner, they [emigrants] were less than a box of goods, and handled with less care." The agents were responsible for accommodating the passengers. In parceling out space, and to maximize profits, they usually packed people in with no regard for sex, age, or health. Food, bedding, and baggage were often filthy, and inadequate ventilation and sanitation added to the discomfort. The headroom rarely reached more than six feet high, and little fresh air came in because windows were usually closed at night and during poor weather, creating a "miasma." The result, noted Kapp, was that a transatlantic crossing was "an enterprise requiring more than ordinary courage." Kapp went so far as to argue that white passengers were actually worse off than slaves because, as property, slaves were more valuable to their owners. Of course, this discounts several very important distinctions: immigrants left their homes voluntarily and were not chained or force-fed on board ship. And conditions for immigrants did improve: by the antebellum era, North American passage mortality rates, although still high, had fallen to about 10 percent annually.[29]

Nonetheless, when the Mullers were traveling, sickness and death were an ever-present concern. The most prevalent problem was seasickness, which could be quite serious. Combined with food that was nutritionally imbalanced and inadequate fresh water, seasickness could lead to malnutrition, dehydration, and thus increased susceptibility to disease. Contemporary accounts generally referred indiscriminately to fevers. These included illnesses such as typhus (known as ship fever), typhoid, smallpox, cholera, and dysentery. According to historian Thomas Page, "An old-fashioned sailing vessel, once visited by the typhus, cholera, or smallpox, often carried the germs of contagion for years." [30]

Illness and malnutrition, then, went hand in hand. Although the Mullers may have sufficiently provisioned themselves for the journey, their supplies were exhausted before the ocean voyage even began, making them dependent upon the captain for sustenance. [31] Although the passenger list and information about the Mullers' arrangements have not survived, the example of the ship *Elizabeth* indicates what their captain might have agreed to provide:

Sunday—1 lb. beef, 1/2 lb. rice

Monday—1 lb. flour

Tuesday—1/2 lb. pork with pease

Wednesday—1 lb. beef and barley

Thursday—1/2 lb. pork with pease

Friday—1 lb. flour

Saturday—1 lb. beef and barley

per week—1 lb. butter, 1 lb. cheese, 6 lbs. bread

per day—1 glass gin, 3/4 gallon water

Also provided was a "sufficient quantity of vinegar to cleanse vessel and refresh passengers." Because they had paid no fare, children were allotted no rations of their own and had to be fed from the adult rations. This would have been a strain on the Mullers, with three children (not including the baby, who was probably still nursing.) Emigrants were expected to cook their own food, usually making use of two small (five-by-four feet) galleys. [32]

Since the Mullers were no longer considered paying customers, they were in particular jeopardy. An account of German redemptioners arriving at Perth Amboy, New Jersey, in 1805 gives some idea of what the Mullers and their compatriots may have suffered on their journey. Members of the German Society of Philadelphia, organized to assist immigrants to that city, met the ship, the *General Wayne,* and reported what they encountered. The society agent's report was blunt: "I went to visit those unfortunate people, and in truth they may be called unfortunate. And I must confess I have seen a number of vessels at Philadelphia with redemptioners, but never did I see such a set of miserable beings in my life. Death, to make use of the expression, appeared to be staring them in the face." The *General Wayne*'s passengers had a variety of complaints about their treatment on the journey. At port in Tonningen, they had contracted with the captain to be transported to New York and to receive a certain amount of food on the voyage. After leaving the port, they sailed to Portsmouth, England, where they remained for one month during which time the captain endeavored to coerce the men to enlist in the British army, threatening them with starvation and whipping. After they sailed, he made good on his threats: twenty-five people died of starvation on the voyage. The society planned to prosecute the captain.[33]

Other groups met a similar fate. The *Niles' Register* recounted the abuse suffered by immigrants traveling in 1817 and 1818, the same time as the Mullers. In November 1817, the Baltimore newspaper reported that there were "very distressing accounts of the state of German immigrants attempting to reach the United States through the ports of the Netherlands." These accounts noted the deaths of passengers from disease and starvation, some while languishing in European ports.[34] On January 31, 1818, the *Register* depicted a situation strikingly similar to that of the Mullers'. More than one thousand people left Amsterdam on the *April*, but only about five hundred arrived alive at the port of New Castle, Delaware. Those unable to pay passage were being detained, some of them "in the most deplorable condition," including children who had been orphaned on the voyage. At least part of their distress was caused by the fact that some passengers were forced to await sailing at Amsterdam for "a considerable time, and, owing to bad food and poor attendance, those on board were, more or less, sick and full of vermin," according to the report of Henry T. Vierhaus, secretary of the German Society of Philadelphia.[35] About three hundred of the survivors were then advertised as redemptioners in the Wilmington newspaper, *American Watchman*.[36]

Also about to be advertised as redemptioners, although their fares had already been paid in full, were the Mullers and their fellow passengers. They had come on three Dutch ships, the *Emmanuel*, the *Johanna Maria,* and the *Juffer Johanna* (the Mullers on this last), sailing in December 1817. A journey of about ninety days brought them to the Balize, the pilot station at the mouth of the Mississippi River, on March 6, 1818.[37]

Twenty-five years later in court, when asked to recall their voyage across the Atlantic, those traveling with the Mullers did not provide detailed accounts. Given the horror of their nearly year-long journey, many had erased the painful memories from their minds and did not want to recall the event. Mortality statistics, however, indicate that conditions were horrific. According to Francis Schuber, "on account of want or scarcity of provisions, a great many of the passengers died."[38] How many exactly is undetermined. Schuber remembered that eight hundred people had left Holland, while J. Hanno Deiler, a Tulane University professor of German who wrote about the case in 1889, put the number at eleven hundred. The discrepancy is at least partly explained by the fact that Deiler noted that eleven hundred people were originally scheduled to be transported on a large Russian ship, the *Rudolph*. When those passengers were reassigned to three smaller ships, not all the travelers apparently made the transfer, though Deiler assumed they had. Francis Schuber said that about eight hundred people were on the original ship, yet only about seven hundred left on the three ships that sailed. Whether those one hundred died before the ships departed, found other means of transportation, or simply gave up and returned home is unclear. Schuber's figure is likely the more accurate because he acted as steward on the trip, dispensing supplies, and thus possessed a list of the passengers for his ship, the *Juffer Johanna*, and knew directly how many sailed on board one ship.[39]

On March 6, 1818, according to the *Louisiana Gazette*, the three ships discharged 597 German passengers at New Orleans.[40] The ships had arrived at the Balize together and now sailed close enough for the passengers to call across to one another. It was at this time that friends and family on board the *Johanna Maria* and the *Emmanuel* learned that Dorothea Muller and her baby Daniel had not survived the journey.[41] Far from home in a foreign land, exhausted, malnourished, and ill, mourning the loss of their mother and infant brother, the surviving Mullers—father Daniel, children Jacob, Dorothy, and Salomé—probably found little cause to celebrate their arrival. But they likely experienced at least a sense of relief at the end of the long sea voyage. To walk on dry land and breathe fresh air would have meant a great deal after their winter confinement of so many months. Perhaps the family even resolved to put their pain aside and look with hope to the future, the chance to start over, albeit diminished in number. But as terrible as their last several months had been, life for the Muller family was about to get even worse. Their choice of a new home had been taken from them, and they had been deposited thousand of miles from that destination. Now they found their personal freedom in danger as well. Although the Mullers and their fellow travelers had already paid the price of their transport to this country, they soon found themselves sold into indentured servitude.

CHAPTER 3

New Orleans

⟨⟩

Germans constituted the second-largest class of immigrants (after the British) to the United States in the eighteenth and nineteenth centuries.[1] Many, like the Mullers, chose Philadelphia as their ultimate destination. Throughout the eighteenth century this city had been the primary port of entry into the colonies, surpassed only by New York after 1816.[2] Philadelphia was a location especially popular with Germans, who formed communities in parts of the city and in the countryside around Lancaster. The Mullers and their fellow travelers, however, were taken not to Philadelphia but to New Orleans, more than a thousand miles south. A more different location would have been hard to imagine. New Orleans in 1818 had spent less than two decades in American hands since the Louisiana Purchase; in many ways it was still a European colonial outpost. Residents spoke French, street signs were in French and Spanish, and even the legal system bore the stamp of the Roman civil code more than English common law. Philadelphia, a large, sophisticated, prosperous port, had once served as the nation's capital and still retained its distinctive Quaker influence. New Orleans, by contrast, was by turns a backwater and a boom town whose population had doubled in the decade after American acquisition. This population was diverse; particularly novel to European eyes was the large number of black and mixed-race residents. Situated in a swamp, the city was unhealthy in the extreme.[3]

The Muller family and their shipmates' first sight of American land was at the Balize, the pilot station at the mouth of the Mississippi River.[4] Navigating the delta was challenging because no completely satisfactory channel ran from the Gulf of Mexico into the river. Sandbars and sediment limited the size of vessels serving the harbor at New Orleans; ships frequently ran aground and might remain stuck for weeks. When not on the water, the pilots lived in a small cluster of shacks at the base of the lighthouse marking the southeast pass. As historian Joseph Tregle, Jr., has described it, "No spot on earth was more desolate and lonely than the Balize in the early part of the nineteenth century."[5]

FIGURE 5. "View of the Balize, at the Mouth of the Mississippi, January 7, 1819," by Benjamin Henry Latrobe. *Courtesy of the Maryland Historical Society.*

The first sight of land in three months, then, offered less than a warm welcome to weary travelers. The banks of the lower Mississippi must have appeared abandoned to Europeans accustomed to waterways edged by cities, villages, and farmland under cultivation. But those feeling well enough to go out on deck and look at the scenery might have been captivated by the strange appearance of their new environment. Even in December, in winter, everything along the river was lush and green.

Several voyagers who took the trip upriver at about the same time as the Mullers provide a picture of what visitors to New Orleans encountered en route to the city. Benjamin Henry Latrobe, engineer of the famed Philadelphia waterworks, arrived in 1819 to oversee construction of what was to be his last project, the New Orleans waterworks.[6] Duke Paul of Württemberg, nephew of King Frederick, was twenty-five when he first traveled to the United States in 1822. Keenly interested in natural science and geographical exploration, his account of the physical world is detailed in the extreme.[7] German cousins Emil and Julius Mallinckrodt arrived in

1831 from Dortmund, Prussia, and continued upriver to establish a farm in Missouri.[8]

Upon entering the mouth of the Mississippi from the Gulf of Mexico, travelers noticed numerous log islands—what Duke Paul referred to as *embarras* the Creole term for masses of tree trunks, uprooted by erosion, which became entangled, creating floating rafts. Over time these built up at the river's mouth, creating ever-narrower channels. Because of the embarras and sandbanks and shallows, piloting the mouth of the Mississippi was a delicate task. Only the river's main outlet where the Balize stood was navigable by large vessels.[9]

Latrobe and Duke Paul described the Balize as a collection of wooden houses built on piles driven into the water and mud, with two lookout towers used by the pilots to spot ships entering the channel. The Balize was also the first customs station that travelers encountered, and it was here that officers came on board ship to check the cargo. Duke Paul found the "forlorn station of the pilots" particularly dismal: "Nature seems to have destined this desolate region solely for the habitation of giant reptiles and countless mosquitoes." He depicted the Balize as "a little place subject to all the hardships of a most unhealthy, swampy, and entirely unhospitable region, and presenting a scene of greatest privation, where man subjects himself to hardship for the sake of gain. A stay in the hot season becomes unbearable because of the clouds of tormenting insects and incessant croaking of frogs on the lower banks of the Mississippi."[10]

It was a little over one hundred miles from the Balize to New Orleans, a trip that took Emil and Julius Mallinckrodt two days. They reported lowering anchor at the mouth of the Mississippi and then being towed upriver to the city, along with three other ships, by a steamboat.[11] The first steamboat, actually named *New Orleans,* had appeared on the river in 1812; such craft soon became a more common sight. In 1818, the *Louisiana Gazette* noted that steamboats had "ceased to be a novelty," but they had yet to reach their heyday in the 1840s and 1850s.[12] Arriving in late December, the Mallinckrodts saw that "On the lower Mississippi everything is green and in bloom. Plane trees [sycamores], trees of life, a curious kind of oak, azaries [azaleas?], and a mixture of the most various foliage form a forest which does not yet have an owner."[13]

Gradually, as travelers ventured up the lower river, plantations became more frequent sights. Most of them grew rice, while sugarcane became common about fifty miles upriver from the Balize. Although blocked somewhat from view by the levée which ran all the way to the city, enough was visible for the Mallinckrodts to note how crops seemed to flourish in this unusual environment. All the visitors commented on two things obviously foreign to them: the abundance of waterfowl and alligators and the orange groves.[14] The next landmark was the English Turn, a great bend in the river fifteen miles below New Orleans. There stood a quarantine station, used only sporadically. On Duke Paul's journey, a doctor came on board briefly to check the passengers for disease. But Duke Paul pointed out the inefficacy of this procedure since the ship had already made contact with people below river who were not quarantined.[15]

These sojourners undoubtedly saw many of the same things the Mullers would have observed because all encountered New Orleans at about the same time. In addition, the three travelers who were Germans likely saw the city from a perspective similar to that of the Mullers. They were, however, considerably better situated economically than the impoverished Muller family was. Duke Paul, as a member of a prominent royal family, traveled in luxury. Even though he had fallen on hard times (the New Orleans waterworks was his biggest project in many years), Benjamin Latrobe could afford a cabin on board. And the Mallinckrodt brothers, while immigrants, had saved enough money to travel in relative comfort, also in a cabin. The difference in perspective between this class of traveler and passengers like the Mullers is illustrated by the words of Duke Paul: "The first sight of land brings elation to every seafarer. This impression is so much greater on that traveler whose imagination had busied himself in advance with a fantasy of a world entirely new to him."[16] For the Mullers, the trip had been more nightmare than fantasy.

The three ships carrying the Mullers and their compatriots arrived at the Balize together. While they waited for a pilot to guide them upriver, passengers went up on deck and began calling to friends on the other ships, exchanging news. After a horrific three-month voyage, the topic of conversation on most lips was who among them had not survived.[17] But they had little time to dwell on their losses, for they were soon disembarking in the city.

New Orleans, at the time of the Mullers' arrival in 1818, was a city in transition. In American hands only since 1803, it bore the vestiges of the old colonial regimes, French and Spanish, as well as the evidence of fresh American development. As David Goldfield has described it, "Its frontier scruffiness vied with French insouciance as the dominant feature of its lifestyle." Yet the city's apparent lack of sophistication belied its emerging status as a center of worldwide shipping. By 1821, Lloyd's of

London predicted that New Orleans was on its way to becoming the world's greatest port.[18]

The city had been hard-hit by the 1807 Embargo Act, which prompted a precipitous drop in the volume of imports and exports. Weeks after Louisiana achieved statehood in April 1812, the United States went to war with Britain. The British initiated a blockade of the Mississippi, virtually halting all trade. New Orleans became more directly involved in the War of 1812 after the peace treaty had been signed but before news of this development had reached American and British forces there. The Battle of New Orleans resulted in an American victory over a numerically stronger British army.[19]

With the war's end, the New Orleans waterfront was once again bustling as business returned to the city. German immigrant and river trader J. G. Flügel counted four hundred ships in port just in the month of February 1817. Fourteen years later, the Mallinckrodt brothers put the number closer to one thousand.[20] The variety of vessels was equally impressive. Flatboats and small vessels tied up and discharged cargo at the Custom House, increasingly competing for space with steamboats, while oceangoing vessels docked below.[21]

FIGURE 6. "New Orleans from the Lower Cotton Press, 1852." *Courtesy of the Historic New Orleans Collection, accession no. 1947.20.*

The city extended one and a quarter miles along the river and a half-mile inland. To Europeans accustomed to ancient, developed cities, downtown New Orleans appeared very much like a country town, only larger. New Orleans had been a walled and fortified site until 1804, when the Americans began demolishing the forts; however, parts of the earthenwork walls, collapsing from disrepair, remained. Beyond the crumbling walls lay swampland. Across the river (what is now the borough of Algiers) stood the plantation homes of the Duverjé, LeBoeuf, and Verret families.[22]

The original town, or French Quarter, had been laid out in 1721 with, according to historian John Kendall, "mathematical exactitude" in a grid pattern of narrow streets. As the population grew, residents did not simply expand outward from the existing town. Instead, they established small, separate settlements along the city's edge with their own street systems. Over time these became fused to the downtown area and to each other. Author Harold Sinclair likened these newer sections of city to "gold-rush camps."[23]

The French Quarter (Vieux Carré, or original square) was filling up by the late eighteenth century. A survey done in 1822 indicated that New Orleans had 1,436 brick and 4,401 wooden houses, plus warehouses, shops, and other public buildings. Many structures were new in 1818 since major fires in 1788 and 1794 had necessitated extensive rebuilding. The first conflagration destroyed nearly the entire city; the second ruined more than one thousand houses. Afterward, rebuilding gave the city a denser quality, with fewer yards and gardens and more buildings fronting sidewalks with common walls or alleys in between. House plans were simple: two rooms in the front, two in the back, and separate kitchens or servants quarters in the courtyard. Many houses had French doors and heavy, solid shutters, which could be closed against the heat of a summer's day or for protection at night.[24]

Public buildings included a Catholic church, an Ursuline convent, a monastery, and a charity hospital. There was also a government house, a district court, an army barracks, and a prison. The Custom House, two banks, and numerous stores served the business sector. Many of these businesses fronted on or were near the city's most prominent square, the Place d'Armes, site of the cathedral, while others were located on the river. The Custom House, built from a design by architect Benjamin Latrobe, was a small, simple structure of Pennsylvania brick with stone trim. One of the first examples of classical revival architecture in the city, its poor foundation caused decay to set in almost immediately; and the building was demolished in 1819, shortly after Latrobe's and Salomé Muller's arrival in the city.[25]

Prominent along the waterfront was the levée, the city's commercial heart. A low embankment of earth, about four feet high and fifteen feet wide, the levée was built to protect the city against flooding and dated from the city's initial construction in the 1720s. Called by visitor Henry Breckenridge "the most considerable work of art yet constructed for the purpose of rendering this country habitable," the levée began north of the city, one hundred and fifty miles upstream near the town of Pointe Coupée. In the city the levée was where produce was sold and inhabitants took their evening walks. The French Market was situated on Levée Street, near the Place d'Armes and, according to tradition, the site of an old Choctaw trading place. The Halle des Boucheries (the Meat Market) was erected in 1813 to replace an earlier market destroyed by a hurricane in 1811. Built with a low-pitched tile roof and open-arcaded walls of plastered brick, it held more than one hundred stalls. The Halle des Legumes (the Vegetable Market) was added in 1822. The market spilled out into the streets near the levée, and the whole area filled with sellers bringing their produce to market.[26]

Activity along the levée represented the local manifestation of a burgeoning international trade. The city's economy had been rapidly growing toward the end of the eighteenth century, along with that of the rest of the Louisiana Territory. In 1795 a treaty between Spain and the United States allowed Americans to deposit goods in New Orleans without charge. As a result, port traffic increased greatly, and many Americans began settling in northern Louisiana. That same year, sugarcane was introduced by planter Etienne Boré (later mayor of New Orleans from 1803 to 1804), and sugar production soon dominated plantation agriculture. Until that time, Louisiana's economy had been mixed: it included cattle raising and the growing of indigo and tobacco.[27]

By 1818, visitor Estwick Evans called the city "a place of immense business" and surmised that in fifty years it would probably be the greatest port in the world. Ships came from abroad with cash to purchase a variety of goods, with the result, Evans claimed, that there was probably more specie in circulation there than anywhere else in the world. Oceangoing vessels arrived each November to purchase cotton. Shipping peaked in the spring, when it was common to see large vessels four deep, a quarter mile below the city, surrounded by hundreds of river craft. According to Evans, "vast quantities of provisions of every kind" came from the nation's interior, down the Mississippi and its tributaries, where it was sold to the people of New Orleans, to captains for ship stores, and for distribution to foreign markets. These products included stone, coal, flour, corn, wheat, oats, hay, lard, hams, bacon, barreled pork, lumber, hides, beef, stoneware, lead, potatoes, cider, cheese, rum, whisky, and salt. Smaller quantities of goods came from Europe—silks, linen, wine, china, silverware. All this cargo piled up on top of the levée, sometimes sitting there for weeks. Eventually the city acted to prevent this practice. Cargo left for more than one week was taken to a municipal warehouse, and owners had to pay a fee to claim their goods.[28]

As vigorous as the city's economy was, its health was poor. Yellow fever was a frequent visitor, returning persistently if not annually. The summer after the Mullers' arrival, an epidemic killed some two thousand residents. After an earlier outbreak in 1811, the city had enjoyed a six-year respite, but the disease returned in 1817. Winter brought an end to that attack, and the following year saw no large outbreak, although a few cases of smallpox were recorded. (Smallpox was generally kept in check by vaccines, although not everyone was vaccinated.) Yellow fever returned in full force in 1819. Exact figures are not available, but conservative estimates put the death toll at about two thousand. Outbreaks continued. Timothy Flint, a Congregational minister from Massachusetts who visited the city in 1822, noted that "the hearse is seen passing the streets at all hours."[29]

Newcomers to the city were particularly at risk. Amos Stoddard observed that "strangers, much more than natives, are apt to fall victim to the epidemics of the country, particularly the boatmen from the Ohio. Those unaccustomed to the climate and of intemperate habits, exposing themselves to the heats and dews, are sure to experience dangerous maladies." Duke Paul recalled hearing upon his arrival in December 1822 that many Germans had recently succumbed to yellow fever. Fellow German visitor Karl Pöstl also learned that hundreds of Germans had died of the fever between 1814 and 1822. He described an alarming scene: "Whole streets in the upper suburb (inhabited chiefly by Americans and Germans) were cleared of their inhabitants, and New Orleans was literally one vast cemetary [*sic*]."[30]

Benjamin Latrobe was one such unfortunate newcomer. His son, Henry, directing operations on the waterworks, was struck down by yellow fever in 1817. Latrobe came to New Orleans in 1819 to take over the construction and was himself felled by the disease the following year, dying on the third anniversary of his son's death. Latrobe's death is particularly ironic because the waterworks he was creating were designed to reduce standing water (a breeding ground for disease-bearing mosquitoes), provide fresh water, and enable the city's streets to be cleaned regularly.[31]

Immigrant guidebooks warned people away from the city between May and October, the yellow fever season. But public officials avoided effecting a quarantine because they wanted an open port. Pressure from shipping and mercantile interests kept genuine reform at bay. Until 1817 virtually nothing was done in terms of a quarantine to protect New Orleans from communicable disease. Mayor Augustin Macarty and the City Council finally initiated quarantine laws after June 1817, when yellow fever attacked, but their action came too late to have an impact. The city established a Board of Health the following spring. This new agency promptly proclaimed a quarantine on all ships coming up the Mississippi and established a quarantine station at the Balize, with a full-time doctor and hospital.[32]

Positive results were not immediately apparent, however, both because of conflict between the Board, the City Council, and the state legislature and because of the especially unsanitary conditions in New Orleans. Like most urban areas, the city had problems with runoff from gutters, garbage collecting in the streets, and waste from local industries such as butcher shops; but New Orleans, because of its elevation below sea level, had additional challenges. Dr. J. M. Picornell wrote a pamphlet describing these problems, calling the city's yards "places of horror." Both Picornell and Latrobe recounted seeing gravediggers gouge holes in coffins to let gases escape, which allowed the coffins to sink into water-filled graves. Timothy Flint added that "one of the circumstances dreadful to the imagination of a sick stranger, is the probability of being buried in the water." [33]

The Board of Health saw itself as "David advancing upon Goliath," according to medical historian John Duffy. The City Council, however, was apparently annoyed that the new Board had taken some of the Council's power and therefore refused to cooperate in enforcing regulations and providing funding for the Board's initiatives. By March 1819, the state legislature had abolished the Board and its regulations and ordered the sale of the quarantine station, although, to appease the minority, the governor was given the authority to establish quarantine in the future if he chose. He did reestablish the station in 1820 in response to an outbreak of yellow fever. His action came too late, however, for by July the city was in the grip of a major epidemic.[34]

By 1822, the *New Orleans City Directory* was claiming the enactment of a quarantine as one of the Board of Health's greatest accomplishments;

but by 1825, anti-quarantine forces, bolstered by the apparent inability of quarantine to prevent yellow fever recurrences, had again persuaded the legislature to abolish the Board and dispose of the all quarantine stations. Total quarantine was not brought about until the 1850s, after an epidemic of the disease killed some eight thousand people in the city. And not until 1861, when the port was blockaded by the Union army, did New Orleans enjoy its first complete respite from yellow fever.[35]

Despite the constant threat of disease, or perhaps because of it, New Orleanians enjoyed a rich social life. Not all visitors, however, viewed this aspect of the city in a positive light. Estwick Evans, writing about his 1818 visit, claimed that "Dissipation in New Orleans is unlimited. Here men may be vicious without incurring the ill opinion of those around them:—for all go one way." He qualified his statement by adding that "New Orleans is much less corrupt, in many particulars, than it used to be." Evans attributed this moral improvement to increasing American influence. Another visitor, William Darby, put it more positively and succinctly: "There are few places on earth where human life can be enjoyed with more pleasure, or employed to more pecuniary profit."[36]

Amusements ranged from the formal and elaborate (theater performances and masked balls) to the casual (visits to taverns and gambling houses.) By 1810, the city boasted at least three theaters, with performances in French and English. At least one visitor, however, was not impressed with New Orleans's cultural offerings. Writer Karl Pöstl complained that the American theater was attended by only the lowest class of Americans and that "the pieces are execrably performed." The quality of the performance was reflected for Pöstl in the theater's physical surroundings: "The curtain consists of two sailcloths, and the horrible smell of whiskey and tobacco is a sufficient drawback." Attracting a higher, or at least wealthier, class, were fancy dress balls. Public balls had been held twice weekly during Spanish rule, and the practice was carried on after American acquisition. The first quadroon ball, held soon after in 1805, initiated the system of *plaçage* in which white men kept light-skinned mistresses of mixed racial descent. By the antebellum era, balls of various kinds had become extremely popular. This was particularly true for public masquerades, which drew a wide range of races and classes.[37]

Bars were abundant in New Orleans. Arriving on a Sunday, Karl Pöstl was surprised to find shops open, while the "coffee-houses, grog-shops and *estaminets*, as they are called, of the French and German inhabitants, exhibited a more noisy scene." The number of bars in the city grew by more than

70 percent between 1825 and 1830. Joseph Tregle, Jr., has written that "probably no community in the world revolved so much around its grog shops, cabarets, gambling dens, circus pits, and theaters" as did New Orleans. But according to John Kendall, antebellum New Orleans was "preeminently a sporting town." Estwick Evans agreed, calling the number of gambling houses "almost innumerable."[38]

When gambling was still illegal in 1802, the city had imported 54,000 packs of playing cards—more than four each for every resident and visitor. According to historian Thomas Ingersoll, gambling seemed to "have reached the level of a mania in New Orleans by the 1820's." The legislature soon began efforts at regulation. In 1823, it authorized the establishment of six gambling houses and required each to pay five thousand dollars for the benefit of the Charity Hospital and the College of Orleans. By the 1830s, Davis's Ball Room, located behind St. Louis Cathedral, offered a variety of choices for a gambler, including keno, twenty-one, faro, monte, roulette, and craps. Cheaper establishments, not to mention street corners, provided opportunities for everyone, the poor as well as the rich, to try his or her luck. Even the respectable gambled, and lotteries were widespread, especially among churches.[39] James P. Thomas, an African-American boy who left his Nashville home to see the world, was impressed by the diversity of gambling options. One day he passed an elegant house that hosted a group of wealthy white politicians, and the next day he visited the Louisiana Cockpit on Dumaine Street. There he lost two dollars betting on cock fighting. Neither his youth nor race precluded his participation. Thomas noted in his diary the diversity and at least temporarily egalitarian nature of the crowd. He observed that people of all races and classes mingled and won and lost together.[40]

In addition to its variety of less-than-wholesome amusements, visitors also depicted New Orleans as a city filled with crime. Traveler J. G. Flügel, writing in his journal in 1817, noted that ten o'clock in the evening was "a rather dangerous time to pass over the levee, since so many persons have been assaulted there and several murdered." Another entry recounted the assault and robbery of a man in the street: "Such cases are heard of every day and one must be careful." Estwick Evans concurred, writing that "murders here are frequent, and sometimes not enquired into."[41]

Scholars, however, have questioned this perception of New Orleans as a particularly dangerous city. The exact crime rate remains unknown because criminal court records no longer exist. But according to Thomas Ingersoll, "there is no reason to suppose that rates were higher than in

American cities of the same size." Historian Liliane Crété noted that street lights were installed in 1796. Oil lamps suspended from chains at street corners were lit every evening at sundown. Perhaps partly because of this, she has argued that New Orleans was a "fairly peaceable town." The police force, with some forty watchmen, spent most of its time seeking out fugitive slaves, ensuring that bars and their patrons obeyed the law, and monitoring the speed limit for horse-drawn vehicles.[42]

The police force was needed largely to cope with a rapidly growing population. Soon after it came into American hands, New Orleans experienced the first of two population explosions. The city's population had doubled between the years 1805 and 1810 and then doubled again in the 1830s, mainly due to Irish and German immigration.[43] By 1814, New Orleans was the nation's sixth-largest city, with 17,242 residents.[44]

What was most noticeable to visitors was the population's diversity. Benjamin Latrobe was especially struck by it: "On arriving at New Orleans in the morning, a sound more strange than any that is heard any where else in the world astonishes. It is a more incessant, loud, rapid and various gabble of tongues of all tones that was ever heard at Babel. It is more to be compared to the sounds that issue from an extensive marsh, the residence of a million or two of frogs, from Bull frogs up to Whistlers than to any thing else." William Darby noted that "No city perhaps on the globe, in an equal number of human beings, presents a greater contrast of national manners, language, and complexion, than does New Orleans." Estwick Evans commented that "Perhaps no place in the world, excepting Vienna, contains a greater variety of the human race than New Orleans." He went on to note that, besides the foreign population, there was a great variety of people of color, including "commixtures not yet classified."[45] It was of course the classification of an individual's race that was at the heart of the Sally Miller case.

CHAPTER 4

Germans and Redemptioners

ㅤ

$\mathcal{T}$he Mullers, despite their consider-
able hardships, were at least not alone in this strange place. By the early
nineteenth century, New Orleans had attracted a sizable and cohesive
German community. Like the French, Spanish, and Irish, the Germans had
separate residential neighborhoods and institutions and retained use of their
own language, as evidenced by the great number of foreign-language newspapers available in the city.[1] Like the Mullers, many of these Germans had
come to America as redemptioners, a little-known form of indentured servitude practiced in the eighteenth and nineteenth centuries, and had served
out their terms to become free citizens of New Orleans.

New Orleans's Germans usually lived in what was then the separate
city of Lafayette, located downriver from the American section.[2] Growth
came from a steady stream of immigrants, especially Germans and Irish.
The rear of the city (now the Garden District) was occupied by well-to-do
merchants, while poorer immigrants and boatmen lived near the river.
Along the waterfront, in an area called Bull's Head, were the slaughter-
houses. Cattle came from Texas and were penned at the foot of St. Mary's
Street, where Francis Schuber plied his trade as a butcher. Industries related
to cattle, such as tanning and rendering, filled part of the bustling riverfront;
and of course, cotton and other plantation products were shipped there, too.
As was true of many immigrants throughout history, Germans clustered in,
or were forced into, a few occupations. One traveler in the late 1820s, for
example, commented that the "watchmen and lamp lighters are Germans."
Germans were prominent on the New Orleans police force and also worked
as butchers, mechanics, and, like many immigrants, hired hands.[3]

Some Germans had entered the United States at New Orleans with the
intention of migrating westward to Texas or up the Mississippi to the
Midwest. *Duden's Report*, promoting emigration to Missouri, went through
three editions and had a tremendous impact in Germany.[4] Gottfried Duden
had lived on a Missouri farm for three years and then returned home to

publicize a glowing account of his experience. Although he was later denounced as *der Lugenhund* ("a lying dog"), his report still carried weight in the 1830s and encouraged many Germans to make the journey to the United States.[5]

Much scholarly attention has been paid to immigrants who went north rather than south, but in fact Germans flocked to the slave states of Louisiana, Texas, Missouri, and Kentucky.[6] Many simply passed through New Orleans, working in the city to raise funds before moving on.[7] Some immigrants booked passage to New Orleans after being falsely persuaded by agents that they could go anywhere from there, particularly South America. Agents also sold fake tickets to inland locations. Some German provinces used New Orleans as a deposit site for "undesirables"; for example, towns in Baden paid passage for one hundred people in 1852. (Each was given $1.20.)[8] Regardless of their intent in coming to New Orleans, by 1850, nearly ten thousand Germans were listed in the city census and almost twenty-five thousand in the state of Louisiana.[9]

The German presence in nineteenth-century Louisiana, then, was not minimal. Nor was it recent. German immigration dates to the 1717 colony established by Scottish land speculator John Law. A professional gambler, Law had left Britain after killing a man in a duel. He became a friend and advisor to Philippe of Orléans, French regent after the death of Louis XIV. Law wanted to populate Louisiana and make himself rich in the process. His plan was to persuade the wealthy to purchase stock in his landholding company and/or buy land in Louisiana themselves. He envisioned enticing or forcing the poor of Europe to provide labor on these lands. After acquiring a supportive governor in Louisiana, Sieur Bienville, Law initiated what has been called a "brilliant, ruthless sales campaign," flooding Europe with handbills offering land, provisions, and transportation to those who would come to the colony. He also promised crops that needed no cultivation as well as gold, pearls, and the absence of disease.[10]

Some ten thousand Germans heeded Law's call, leaving their homes in the Rhine region in 1717. Only about six thousand prospective colonists actually left Europe; the rest died of disease or starvation awaiting passage in French ports. Of those who left the continent, only about two thousand arrived in North America alive. They disembarked at Dauphin Island, near Mobile Bay, and at Biloxi. News of their fate apparently did not spread rapidly, for Germans continued to migrate over the next few years. Another group in 1722 established a settlement near New Orleans along what became known as the German Coast.[11]

Nearly a century after the arrival of these first settlers, the Muller family arrived in New Orleans. Their journey upriver had taken a little more than a week from the Balize. New Orleans newspapers reported that on March 6, 1818, three ships from Amsterdam–the *Juffer Johanna*, the *Johanna Maria*, and the *Emmanuel*—discharged a total of 597 passengers at the Custom House.[12]

Upon arrival in the city, immigrants were preyed on by confidence men and swindlers. Unscrupulous porters, employment agents, and owners of boarding houses besieged bewildered travelers as soon as they disembarked or even sooner (some were allowed to board ship at the Balize) and persuaded the vulnerable travelers to part with money for services promised but never received. Others lost their possessions to outright theft. The voyagers carried their belongings in wooden boxes or crates, the largest of which could be the size of a single-story house. Sometimes damaged in transit, the crates could spill belongings everywhere when hoisted from the ship, facilitating theft.[13]

Legislation to protect travelers was initiated in England in 1803; and while the United States followed with similar laws in 1819, at least one historian has suggested that such attempts failed to make an impact for much of the nineteenth century.[14] More helpful perhaps were privately organized local groups that offered support to immigrants. One such group formed in New Orleans in 1847 to assist immigrants in adjusting to their new environment. Among other activities, the German Society found homes for children orphaned on the journey, helping thirty such children in the first year of the organization's existence. It also warned passengers of the actions of confidence men, advising them to await society agents, who would help them obtain jobs and housing.[15]

Such help, however, came too late for the Mullers, who in fact had much more to worry about than pickpockets. Landing in New Orleans, they were undoubtedly hungry, exhausted, possibly ill, disheartened over the disastrous progress of their voyage, and grieving over the deaths of Dorothea Muller and baby Daniel. They may have been relieved to finally reach their destination, but now even the possibility of a fresh start was taken from them as they were sold into indentured servitude to pay for their ocean passage a second time.

The *Louisiana Gazette* advertised the "sale" of the German immigrants for one week following their arrival in the city:

Mr. Krahnstover, super cargo of the ship Juffrou Johanna, lately arrived from Amsterdam, begs leave to inform the inhabitants of

Louisiana, who may want servants of different ages and sexes, labourers, farmers, gardners, mechanics, etc. that he has brought several Swiss and German passengers that wished to emigrate to the country, which may prove to be very serviceable in their respective capacities. For particulars, apply on board, or at the store of Mr. F. W. Am Ende, Toulouse St.[16]

Such advertisements were common. The trip from the Balize to the city, more than one hundred miles, generally took two to three weeks. During this time, the pending arrival of vessels was announced in newspapers so that interested buyers could come to the landing place near the French Market. Redemptioners were lined up, either on the levée, or on board ship, for examination. Buyers paid the passage costs to the captain or agent and then took the redemptioner to the mayor's office, where a contract was drawn up and signed.[17]

The redemption system is less well known than the practice of indentured servitude that brought many Europeans, especially the English, to the colonies in the early years of settlement. Throughout the colonial era, according to historian Aaron Fogleman, "One word characterized the status of most immigrants—servitude." Prior to the American Revolution, more than half of all immigrants came under some kind of servitude arrangement, creating what Fogleman has called "a complex world of the free and the unfree."[18]

Immigration of indentured servants declined after 1680 as slave importation increased, but the decline was only temporary. After 1720 immigration of servants and importation of slaves both reached record levels. In the 1720s, a new form of servitude, the redemptioner system, developed among German-speaking immigrants. Philadelphia merchants in the immigration trade found that relatives, friends, and former fellow villagers of poor immigrants were often willing to redeem their fare costs. The merchants in Rotterdam and Philadelphia (the ports of embarkation and debarkation, respectively, for most Germans) developed a system in which immigrants signed contracts stating the length of time they had to get in touch with people in Pennsylvania who would pay their passage. If they did not raise the money within that time, the new arrivals were auctioned off as indentured servants. Under the redemptioner system, the length and term of service were negotiable, while the prices for servants (that is, passage costs) were fixed. The term *redemptioner* was used because the person was, after a specified period of time, "redeemed," or freed.[19]

When the American Revolution began, immigration to the American colonies virtually ceased. When it resumed in the 1780s, free immigrants dominated. Americans were increasingly less tolerant of the subordination of white males, and in general, acceptance of indentured servitude was eroding. Germany was the exception: there, indentured servitude remained an important aspect of immigration until 1820, reaching a new peak in the years 1816 and 1817.[20]

Under the redemptioner system, German immigrants bound themselves out for several years' service to pay passage. Most were bound to the captain of the vessel, who then contracted with merchants upon arrival in port. Adults generally served three to six years; children from ten to fifteen years, until they came of age; very young children were surrendered without charge to masters, who had to raise and board them. Most redemptioners worked on farms, but some worked at crafts and in shops.[21]

Redemptioners had to work to pay not only their own passage costs but also those costs of any relative who did not survive the journey but had lived for at least half of it. Thus, debt was inherited. As with slave sales, buyers were under no obligation to keep families together. Anyone was allowed to purchase a redemptioner's contract. According to immigrant Gottlieb Mittelburger, not only did English colonists buy redemptioners, so did German Americans, some of whom were former redemptioners themselves. The number of years that redemptioners served was high, argues historian Günter Moltmann, given the cost of travel from Europe. In 1816–1817, the fare was between sixty-five and eighty dollars. Because an unskilled worker could have earned as much as a dollar a day, masters were paying considerably less than four years' worth of work, although they did provide food, clothing, and housing. But at least some immigrants perceived the future opportunities as outweighing the temporary exploitation. As a group of 1817 emigrants from the town of Weinsberg in Württemberg responded when questioned about their reasons for leaving, "they preferred being slaves in America to being citizens of Weinsberg."[22]

The Mullers and their shipmates, however, had not made the decision to travel as redemptioners; they had in fact paid their passage to the United States in full. According to Tulane professor J. Hanno Deiler's 1889 account, when word of the immigrants' treatment spread throughout New Orleans, residents were so outraged that the ships' captains and sailors dared not set foot on land. Some of the German residents of the city channeled their anger into an attempt to prevent the supercargo from selling the passengers into servitude. A hearing was held, apparently to determine the legality of the passengers' indentures but also possibly investigating the treatment they had received on board ship. Deiler found that "according to the unanimous statement of the survivors, most of the victims had literally been starved and not on account of lack of provisions, but as a result of the greed and atrocity of the captains." The food brought by the passengers had been stored inaccessibly to compel them to pay for additional provisions. They were even forced to purchase water that was filled with worms. This amplified the usual shipboard problem of disease, resulting in extreme loss of life; only a single family survived the voyage fully intact. Even more egregious, the *Juffer Johanna* had actually provided a Philadelphia ship in distress with food and water near the entrance of the Mississippi.[23]

Daniel Muller was among those who gave evidence at a hearing instigated, as J. C. Wagner recalled, by "some old German residents." The passengers' counsel, Edward Livingston, was more than competent: he later went on to serve in the U.S. Congress, as Andrew Jackson's secretary of state, and as ambassador to France.[24] Their other lawyer, in an interesting twist of fate, was Livingston's partner, John Grymes. No record survives of the proceedings, but the result is known. The immigrants ultimately lost their bid for freedom and were bound out as servants, most, according to Wagner, for terms of one or two years. Afterward, as immigrant Francis Schuber related, they "were scattered about like young birds leaving a nest without knowing any thing of each other." [25]

The plight of the immigrants excited sympathy among some residents of New Orleans, but the *Gazette* was unmoved. In a March 14, article entitled "German Redemptioners," the newspaper described its position:

> The public attention has been much occupied the last few days with this description of emigrants that have lately arrived from Amsterdam. The novelty of the circumstances has excited feelings of much interest and many reports, it is believed, have gone abroad, calculated to make a very unfavorable impression as to the usage of these people on the passage, and their introduction here to servitude. It is always gratifying to see public sympathy enlisted on the side of humanity; and it is the glory of our country that the oppressed and poor of all nations find in our Land an asylum of protecting justice; but we ought, at the same time, to guard against any impressions which arise only from our feelings and are not supported either by the existence of fact or the intrinsic welfare of the objects of our consideration. These emigrants have come here under special engagement to redeem their passage either by

voluntary servitude; a practice long sanctioned by the like emigrants to the North. [line missing] . . . [con]siderable portion of the agricultural wealth of Pennsylvania is possessed by characters of this description. That there are many privations and suffering incident to a voyage of this nature, is undeniable, but from the appearance of those people now in our city, we should not conclude that their case has been more than ordinarily so. The servitude they have to submit to here is not of a grievous kind, and probably will leave them more vitally free than the political institutions of their own country in their fullest latitude. They are by this means inducted into a knowledge of this country, its language, and its resources and thereby qualified for a more useful application of their labor and their talents when their terms shall expire.[26]

Farther north, the 1818 immigrants met with more understanding. The *Niles' Register*, a national newspaper published in Baltimore, was strongly affected by their situation and addressed it on more than one occasion. Soon after the immigrants' arrival, the *Register* indicated its sympathy:

The heart is sickened with accounts of the sufferings of emigrants from Germany, making their way to the U.S., through the cold-blooded cruelty and infernal avarice of the masters and owners of passenger ships. We are glad that very few of those guilty are our own countrymen—the actors are chiefly Dutch. Cargoes of emigrants, who had wholly or partially paid their passages to the U.S., after suffering almost starvation on shipboard, have on various pretexts, been landed at Lisbon, or the western islands, etc. and left to perish in strange countries, unless saved by the already overburthened demands on the few that are able to assist them. Some hundreds of Swiss and Germans have also arrived at New Orleans, who have been wretchedly treated. Their case considerably excited the feelings of the citizens of that place.[27]

As the *Register* noted, the Germans had not started their journey with plans to indenture themselves in North America. Such abuses were common in the Atlantic passenger trade. Extortion occurred when travelers were stopped at points along the journey in Europe and forced to pay various fees and taxes. Passengers were charged for checking their baggage, which was then often stolen by people claiming to be porters.[28] Germans, of course, were not the only victims. Exploitation of passengers by agents and ships' captains in Britain had become so extensive by 1822 that the American Chamber of Commerce in Liverpool—a major port of embarkation—initiated an investigation. It was found that captains bargained with passenger brokers to fill their ships beyond capacity, stressing shipboard resources. Immigrants were exposed to various other abuses, the report noted, including being charged for illegitimate taxes and services never rendered.[29] Such practices were common throughout Europe; and the result, according to Farley Grubb, was that "Many emigrants had exhausted their resources escaping starvation by the time they reached Amsterdam [port of embarkation for many continental emigrants], and thus an atypically high percentage had to rely on servitude to pay for the final stage of their escape to America."[30]

In response to these activities, some states began to intervene. Pennsylvania, for example, passed a law in 1818 to protect redemptioners and in 1820 prohibited the system altogether. At the same time the system of indentured servitude, according to Frederick Spletstoser, "took on a particularly ugly aspect in Louisiana between 1815 and 1820." Stimulated by the federal law that prohibited the importation of slaves after 1808, Dutch shipowners and agents sent "runners" through villages in the Palatinate, Alsace, Lorraine, Württemberg, and Baden in search of an alternative source of human cargo. As discussed, residents there had been beset by war and heavy taxation since the time of the French Revolution, and in 1816 and 1817 they endured a severe famine. This famine served as a catalyst, causing many to gamble on new lives in the United States. Ripe targets for unscrupulous transportation agents, these people bound themselves to service for three to eight years in exchange for passage to America. No comprehensive statistics exist as to the numbers who entered into these agreements, but among those who did there is no doubt that mortality rates on the voyages were exceedingly high—as much as 50 percent. New Orleans was not the only port to receive these refugees, but the treatment they endured there was singularly brutal.[31]

As a result, some nineteenth-century authors compared redemptioners to slaves. New York Commissioner of Emigration Friedrich Kapp wrote in 1870, "In short, the whole system was utterly vicious and little better than slavery." J. Hanno Deiler, writing eighteen years later, was even more emphatic: "During the time of his service the redemptioner was a *slave*." Deiler interviewed former redemptioners in Louisiana who indicated that "especially did they suffer from the taunts of the negroes who were glad to see members of the hated white race share with them the yoke of bondage, and openly gave expressions to their malicious joy. That, I was told by old Germans, was the hardest of all for them." Deiler also believed that the numerous accounts of runaway German redemptioners offered evidence of their slavish condition.[32]

Indeed, New Orleans's newspaper advertisements for runaway servants appear remarkably like those for runaway slaves. One from the *Louisiana Gazette* of April 1818, serves as an example:

Ten Dollars Reward

Ran away from the subscriber last evening, Two German Redemptioners, namely:

George Stroule, about 28 years of age, 5 feet, 7 inches high, dark complexion and slender make; had on a blue jacket and grey pantaloons with other clothes of the fashion of his country.

Marianne Mowry, wife of said Stroule, about 30 years of age, nearly as tall as her husband, a little pock marked and dressed in the manner of her country.

The above reward will be paid for securing these redemptioners in jail or bringing them to

Lewis Mageonie
On the Canal, suburb Marigny[33]

German visitor Karl Pöstl, who encountered some of the 1818 immigrants when he visited the city several years later, also referred to them as white slaves. "Thus mixed with the negroes in the same kind of labour, they experience no more consideration than the latter," he wrote but then went on to claim that "their conduct certainly deserves no better treatment. Those who did not escape, were driven away by their masters for their immoderate drinking; and all, with a few exceptions, were glad to get rid of such dregs."[34]

Some city officials were also less than sympathetic toward the immigrants, linking them particularly to increased crime. New Orleans had been isolated during the War of 1812. The restoration of peace in 1815 saw a resurgence in trade and immigration, "including a large element of lawless characters." When Governor Jacques Villeré addressed the legislature in January 1818, he claimed that "The multitude of strangers who crowd here daily, the sensible increase of the population, necessarily occasion a multiplicity of petty offenses." The following month, a number of disturbances occurred, which were attributed to immigrants. Villeré again asked the legislature for assistance in coping with problems caused by the large population of "wholly unprincipled" foreigners. The legislature responded with an act mandating that a ship's master was responsible for providing the city government with information about the immigrants he disembarked. The legislature also created a city Criminal Court with three judges and enacted several harsh laws, including one that made armed robbery a capital crime. After the crackdown, Villeré reported in January 1819 that order had been restored.[35]

At the same time, however, public indignation over the particularly egregious treatment of the 1818 redemptioners impelled the Louisiana legislature to act on their behalf. On March 20, 1818, the legislature passed "An Act for the relief and protection of persons brought into this State as Redemptioners." The law authorized the governor to appoint "discreet and suitable" guardians for any "white persons" coming into the state as redemptioners. These guardians were empowered to board vessels, inquire about the nature of contracts that redemptioners had entered into, report any cruel or unjust treatment to the Attorney General, and institute legal proceedings on the redemptioners' behalf. The law also limited redemptioners under the age of eighteen to service until the age of twenty-one. The governor was authorized to send copies of the act to American consuls in Amsterdam, Hamburg, and "other European ports from which vessels with redemptioners usually sail." The law also explicitly prohibited the purchase of contracts by free people of color and released all redemptioners currently serving time under nonwhite masters.[36]

Soon after this legislation was passed, the market for redemptioners collapsed, never to recover, in all three major ports where the activity had been prominent: Philadelphia, Baltimore, and New Orleans. After 1820 indentured servants no longer represented a significant portion of European migration to America. The end of the redemptioner system came not as a result of legal proscription but as a consequence of market collapse. Several scholars have suggested that American demand for servants fell off, but Farley Grubb argues that the supply of servants had dwindled. Passage costs decreased, and immigrants were increasingly able to get money for passage as European agricultural conditions improved.[37]

But such developments came too late to benefit little Salomé Muller. Upon arrival in New Orleans, she and the surviving members of her family found themselves sold into indentured servitude. Whether in fact most redemptioners truly lived under conditions comparable to slavery is debatable, but Sally claimed that her status as a redemptioner had devolved into actual enslavement. By 1843, when her long-lost compatriots discovered her working at her master's coffeehouse, she—if, indeed, this truly was Salomé Muller—had spent her entire adult life thus far as a Louisiana slave.

CHAPTER 5

Sally and John Miller

※

The German witnesses had told the story of a lost European child. John F. Miller's supporters now offered another story—that of an African American slave girl growing into adulthood in New Orleans. At the time of the trial, Sally was owned by Louis Belmonti. But for most of her adult life, she had been the property of John Miller. From 1822 to 1838, Sally had been in either his possession or his widowed mother's, Sarah Canby. Miller's defenders painted a picture of the two as generous masters and upstanding citizens.[1]

Slavery in a city like New Orleans differed from plantation slavery in significant ways. One distinction was the size of individual owners' holdings. New Orleans Parish was the third-highest slave-owning parish in Louisiana, with more than 18,000 slaves in 1850. But although slaveholding was widespread, urban slaveholders generally had fewer slaves than rural owners did, the majority owning only one or two. In 1830, only 215 New Orleans residents owned more than ten slaves each; twenty owners each were listed as having more than twenty slaves.[2]

Accounts of the level of John Miller's slaveholding vary, but at the height of his wealth, he was clearly a part of the New Orleans elite. One former employee testified that when Miller came to the city in 1807 he brought six "servants" with him. By 1823, he was buying more slaves and had about thirty working for him at his sawmill. Mrs. Ann Kopman, who lived with Sarah Canby in the late 1820s, recalled hearing Canby say that she and her son collectively owned about eighty slaves, putting them at the highest level of slave owning. All Miller's trial witnesses agreed that he was considered very wealthy and owned a great many slaves. The 1830 census shows that Miller owned twenty-six slaves. By 1840, he is listed as having only nine slaves in New Orleans, but this was after he had purchased two sugar plantations in the Attakapas region, which would have necessitated the establishment of a substantial slave labor force there. At this time Miller was also facing bankruptcy proceedings; moreover, sometimes certain slaves were held in his mother's name, so an exact tally is difficult to obtain. But Glenn Conrad, who has documented Miller's rural land ownership, writes that he "must be considered a major plantation owner." Miller himself stated that he had owned "many hundreds of slaves" over a thirty-year period and added that he had freed many of them.[3]

In the Crescent City's slave population, women outnumbered men—the reverse of the ratio in the white population. By at least 1820 female slaves had begun to outnumber males, and by 1860 the difference was striking. In New Orleans, the absence of men of marriageable age was especially marked. This gender imbalance was the result of two factors. Owners tended to sell their young male slaves to plantations where they were needed for heavy physical labor. Unlike plantation owners, few urban slave owners depended on their slaves for income. The labor most city slaves performed was domestic service, considered to be women's work. According to Virginia Meacham Gould, "Slave women in the city, therefore, unlike those on plantations, existed in a world in which their gender-specific skills were highly desirable and in many cases, preferable to those of men." The one exception to this rule was industry: most slaves working in urban industries—iron foundries, gasworks, cotton presses—were men. Most were unskilled, but not all (coopers and carpenters, for example), and most had been hired out by their owners. Slaves were also hired out to the city for building, cleaning, paving, and repairing streets, markets, and the levée.[4]

Milling lumber was one of the trades that employed male slaves. Commercial processing of timber began soon after colonial settlement in Louisiana. New Orleans, with its convenient location at the mouth of the Mississippi River, became the colony's center for the lumber trade. Lumbering was greatly stimulated by the introduction of a steam sawmill in New Orleans in 1802, and by 1810 the city supported twenty-one sawmills. The demand for wood fueled the expansion. According to historian John Eisterhold, "As the fastest growing city in the South during the antebellum period, the city construction trade required the use of massive amounts of lumber." American naval development also necessitated a constant supply of wood. Demand was so high that some sawmills operated continuously.[5]

John Fitz Miller played a part of this growing industry. Like many in New Orleans at this time, Miller was not a native of the city. He had been born in Philadelphia in 1780, the son of John Fitz Miller, Sr., and Sarah Wessel Miller. He moved first to Norfolk, then to New Orleans in 1807, his mother following two years later. Miller first worked at the navy yard and then left in about 1818 to open a block-and pump-maker's shop on Levée

Street, in the Faubourg Marigny. Within a few years, he had established a sawmill nearby (Miller and his mother lived adjacent), and by 1834 he had opened a second mill. He also established himself as a builder during that time. Some examples of his work still survive, including the five row houses that form 630–40 Carondelet Street and a storehouse at 701–3 Tchoupitoulas Street.[6]

As one of Miller's slaves, Sally worked in his New Orleans home as a domestic, particularly attending to Miller's widowed mother, Sarah Canby.[7] Male and female slaves had significantly different work experiences, and this differentiation began in childhood. While slave children in general began working at an early age, girls actually started before boys. Young girls were often put to work minding younger children and babies. It was common for girls to begin working as early as age seven; the majority were employed by age eleven, Sally's age when Miller acquired her. Very wealthy slave owners who owned numerous slaves might assign each of them specific chores, such as cooking, washing, carriage driving, or gardening. But most urban masters owned only one or two slaves, and those slaves performed a variety of tasks. For women, this meant the myriad of domestic tasks required to run a household: cleaning, cooking, sewing, washing, gardening, nursing, child care, table waiting, and personal service. Slaves also ran errands, including marketing. For domestics, hours were long, requiring them to rise at 5:00 A.M. and work until curfew at 9:00 or 10:00 at night; but slaves were really on call all the time. According to court testimony, Sally's duties included typical household chores such as waiting table, cleaning silverware, caring for the children of visitors, and accompanying the elderly Mrs. Canby on shopping trips in town. During much of that time, in fact, Canby was Sally's legal owner. Slaves were more likely to be owned by women in New Orleans than outside the city, and most female slaveholders owned female slaves.[8]

Space was at a premium in antebellum cities; therefore, slaves lived in close proximity to their masters. While field slaves on a large plantation might have enjoyed some privacy from whites in separate slave quarters, urban slaves lived either in rooms in the master's house or in a separate service wing behind the house. The most common housing design put the main residence on or close to the street, with the yard and slave quarters behind it. Houses usually adjoined one of the two houses on either side, with the other side separated by an alley that led to a back courtyard. Many courtyards held slave quarters. These were usually long, narrow, two-story buildings either adjoining the master's house at right angles or placed opposite the house in the back of the yard. The second floor contained the sleeping areas; the first housed the kitchen, storerooms, and sometimes stables. The whole plot, usually no more than fifty by one hundred and fifty feet, was enclosed by a brick wall that centered the slaves' activities on the house and yard and discouraged interaction with the outside world. New Orleans was honeycombed with brick barriers, dividing a block into dozens of individual segments. The result was that urban slaves were surrounded by walls, which physically limited their environment when they were not out on errands. Close quarters also intensified relations between slaves and masters.[9]

Relations between slave and master were a crucial component of the *Miller v. Belmonti* trial. According to legal scholar Ariela Gross, "warranty cases put mastery on trial." It was common practice for defense lawyers to demonstrate their clients' favorable treatment of slaves, and this case was no exception.[10] According to Miller's friends, Sally, like his and his mother's other slaves, was treated well. Jonathan L. Lewis, for example, believed that Miller was "a kind, indulgent master, in fact too much so." Several others used the word "indulgent," and one stated that Miller "spoiled" his slaves. William Turner, Miller's partner at the mill, reported that Miller was such a lenient master that Turner had to punish Miller's slaves himself.[11]

Miller's benevolent treatment of his slaves was also demonstrated by concern for their health. Soon after his purchase of Sally, Miller put her under the care of a Dr. Alexander, who in turn took her to a nurse, a free woman of color named Daphne Crawford. (Nursing was a common occupation for women of color, whose skills were especially valued, partly because they were believed to be immune to yellow fever.) Sally was diagnosed with yellow fever, and she was nursed for about a month at Crawford's home in the Vieux Carré.[12]

Sally was fortunate to survive, for yellow fever was one of the deadliest killers of the nineteenth century. The disease, brought in continually on ships from the Caribbean and Central America, greatly affected port cities with tropical climates like New Orleans. While urban areas were especially vulnerable, rural areas lacked sufficient human and mosquito populations to maintain the disease. This prompted the belief that yellow fever was brought to the city by immigrants. Bennett Dowler, a leading physician of his day, who studied the course of yellow fever in Louisiana, stated that "yellow fever is emphatically the strangers' fever." He added that the problem was worsened by the New Orleans's lust for wealth, which outweighed all other considerations of life. Some efforts had been made to control the spread of the disease. In January 1818, Governor Jacques Villeré had asked the legislature to impose a quarantine on the city. The legislature acted in March, giving the governor the authority to establish a quarantine at his discretion. The act's preamble noted that the "disease . . . is principally among strangers lately arrived in this city, and not yet inured to the climate and that many of them are laboring under pecuniary distress." But when few cases appeared that summer, commercial pressure forced the lifting of the quarantine. A severe outbreak followed, which resulted in more than two thousand fatalities. In 1822, the year Sally was a victim of yellow fever, between eight hundred and two thousand people died.[13]

Only complete quarantine would have kept the disease out, and this was unimaginable to a city dependent on trade. Instead New Orleanians adopted a fatalistic acceptance and claimed their city was healthy. Each year, at the beginning of summer, newspapers would ritually announce the absence of illness. Outsiders did not share residents' optimism, and New Orleans became known as the "Necropolis of the South" because of the recurring outbreaks of yellow fever. Between 1796 and 1850, the city saw some cases each year, with major outbreaks every fifteen or twenty years. Four serious epidemics occurred in the 1850s. Minnesota's Bishop Henry Whipple, visiting during one of the epidemics, commented that, "instead of wondering that the yellow fever visits the city, you wonder why it is not here all the time."[14]

Given this harsh reality, one wonders why John Miller was willing to pay for month-long nursing care for a slave he had just purchased. It is possible, of course, that he was simply protecting his investment. Some scholars have also argued that owners of fewer slaves were possibly more benevolent in their treatment than were large-scale planters. Interacting closely on a daily basis theoretically made it more difficult for masters to dehumanize their slaves.[15]

Closer interaction, however, meant more scrutiny from owners. Urban slaves faced numerous restrictions on their mobility. A curfew kept them off the streets after nine in the evening, before dawn, and on Sundays. They were forbidden to congregate in numbers, ride in public vehicles, or play cards with whites or free colored people. But the laws were infrequently enforced. Because city slaves were often hired out, they retained a certain amount of autonomy, many of them working as street peddlers with little supervision. In fact, scholars have noted that slaves and free blacks in New Orleans enjoyed a freedom of movement and association unheard of in rural locations. Newspapers recorded constant complaints against slaves congregating, gambling, and associating with whites and free blacks. Women especially found a chance to communicate while out on regular shopping trips for their masters. One witness in the *Miller v. Belmonti* trial, H. B. Stringer, who had lived with Miller for nearly two years, stated that Sally "went out whenever she liked."[16]

It is not known whether Sally took part in what was perhaps a unique vehicle for socializing: weekly gatherings in an area called Congo (now Armstrong) Square. Situated on the edge of a swamp just across Rampart Street from the French Quarter, the name comes not from the slaves' origin, as early scholars surmised, but from the fact that the square became the regular location for the seasonal appearance of the Congo Circus after 1816. For most of its history, Congo Square was an open field with a few trees rather than a public square laid out by planners. In French colonial days there had been a market where slave vendors sold their wares. Slaves and free blacks gathered there on Sundays, dancing until dusk to the music of African drums and rattles. The *Code Noir* had exempted slaves from forced labor on religious holidays. Southern slaves generally were granted Sundays off but in French Louisiana, slaves were allowed even greater latitude to use that time as they wished. That relaxation of restraint did not disappear when Louisiana came under American rule, although the crowds came mainly from the Creole community rather than the English-speaking black community located uptown.[17]

Benjamin Latrobe, visiting in 1819, reported seeing five to six hundred slaves dancing in Congo Square one Sunday afternoon. Dancers dressed exotically, using bells, ribbons, sashes, and shells. People formed circles with dancers in the center, and each circle had its own musical accompaniment. Musicians used a variety of instruments, including drums and other percussion instruments as well as banjos and violins. Some instruments were clearly improvised. The dances started slowly, gaining in tempo and intensity, building to an ecstatic crescendo when the spent dancers collapsed and were replaced by fresh participants. There was apparently some carryover of African dances and songs, but as the antebellum era progressed and the number of slaves brought directly from Africa dwindled, the African heritage faded.[18]

Some whites were disturbed by the spectacle they had witnessed. John Paxton, in his 1822 New Orleans directory, described the square as the place where "negroes *dance, carouse and debauch on the Sabbath*, to the great injury of the morals of the rising generation" (emphasis original). American southerners, coming to New Orleans after the Louisiana Purchase, were especially appalled by the sight of free blacks mixing with slaves.

Some northern observers were no less judgmental. Latrobe recounted feeling that he had "never seen any thing more brutally savage, and at the same time dull and stupid."[19]

Slaves and free blacks had other outlets for socializing. Grog and grocery shops were common in all southern cities, often allowing mixed gatherings of white and black, slave and free, male and female. They were the center of informal slave life, much to the concern of whites. In New Orleans, the American District just beyond Canal Street became a notorious center of gambling, drinking, and prostitution. Some establishments defied the law to cater to slave customers.[20] On the other hand, Frederick Law Olmsted found mention in a local newspaper of a black area around Baronne Street containing the same respectable establishments as any white neighborhood: a church, a restaurant, coffee houses, an ice cream shop, and a barber shop. Best known as one of the planners of New York City's Central Park, Olmsted traveled throughout the South in the early 1850s, reporting his findings in the *New York Times* and later in book form. During his time in New Orleans, he visited a black church, and his description of the worship makes it sound almost like the activities of Congo Square. Certainly it was livelier and more participatory than what most white northerners would have been accustomed to seeing.[21] All of this meant that urban slaves had opportunities that were unimaginable in rural areas. As Frederick Douglass, who experienced both urban and rural bondage, put it, "A city slave is almost a freeman, compared with a slave on the plantation."[22]

Slaves may have appeared to some to be living as free men and women in New Orleans, but the question in the *Miller v. Belmonti* trial, of course, was whether this particular slave actually *was* a free person. Sally's supporters had given an account of her European origins and journey to this country, but a crucial piece of evidence was missing: the link between Salomé Muller, the girl who went missing in 1818 en route to a farm in northern Louisiana, and the slave Sally who appeared in New Orleans in 1822. The prosecution had not explained how the German child could have come into Mobile slaveowner Anthony Williams's possession. It is possible to imagine that a young orphan unfamiliar with the English language might become indentured to a farmer in an isolated rural area and then be converted tacitly into bondage. Who would protect her rights? The kidnapping of free black children into slavery was not uncommon; it could and did sometimes happen to whites as well. Children kidnapped at a young age were often unable to recall their original free status and were in no position to protest effectively.[23] This scenario was plausible, but Sally and her supporters had been unable to provide any factual evidence for it. Several of the German witnesses recalled hearing that Daniel Muller and his family had been indentured to a farmer in either the Attakapas or Opelousas regions, and John Miller did own property in Attakapas. Beyond this connection, however, the prosecution was unable to offer any information about exactly how Salomé came into Miller's hands.[24]

Miller, on the other hand, provided strong evidence authenticating his legal purchase of his slave Sally. He knew nothing of her origins nor, he asserted, did he need to under the law. The transfer of the girl to Miller occurred at the New Orleans office of notary public Carlile Pollock. The deed of sale indicates that on August 13, 1822, Anthony Williams of Mobile granted John F. Miller power of attorney to sell a "mulatress slave girl named Bridgett of about twelve years of age and light yellow complexion." Miller paid Williams one hundred dollars as an advance. George Pollock and Cornelius Hurst were the witnesses, and they, along with Carlile Pollock, testified at the trial that the document was legitimate.[25]

Sally was fortunate to have escaped the New Orleans slave market, a demeaning and frightening experience for anyone, especially a young girl alone. New Orleans was the South's largest slave market; in 1830, for example, more than four thousand sales occurred.[26] According to Laurence Kotlikoff, between 1804 and 1862, a total of more than 135,000 slaves were sold in New Orleans.[27] Judith Kelleher Shafer's analysis of 1850 slave sales advertised in newspapers also reveals the extent of the booming trade: one-fifth of all slaves in New Orleans were sold each year. The majority were sold at public auction.[28]

The active selling period of the New Orleans market lasted from January to the end of March.[29] Winter was the slack time in agriculture, which allowed for movement of the workforce without disrupting crop production. In addition, disease, particularly yellow fever, flourished in the city's hot, humid summers, so in June the elite left the city, returning in October to resume business.[30] In 1829, the city council had banned the trade from the town center, within the square formed by Canal, Rampart, Esplanade, and Levée streets. But buyers had other options. By the 1850s there were at least twenty-five slave yards, open compounds in which slaves were on view for purchasers, mostly in the section of the Faubourg St. Mary that abutted the Vieux Carré, with some in the Faubourg Marigny on Esplanade Street. Sales occurred there and in the rotundas of the St. Charles and St. Louis hotels, conducted by bilingual auctioneers. By 1860, the New Orleans market had grown large enough to support thirty-four slave traders, not counting the many who traveled into the city to participate in the business.[31]

Large public auctions have captured the public imagination, and in fact they accounted for the majority of New Orleans slave purchases. But sales could also be transacted privately, brokered by go-betweens, buyer and seller having found each other through a newspaper advertisement or merely by word of mouth. Some owners relied on the services of a slave trader, but many white southerners were contemptuous of the profession and the men who practiced it . (Frederic Bancroft, however, argued in his study of the business that slave trading in New Orleans "had a peculiar dash: it rejoiced in its display and prosperity; it felt unashamed, almost proud.")[32] Business for slave traders was good. Prices rose throughout the 1810s, and by 1818 healthy young male slaves were worth a thousand dollars and women only slightly less. But slave prices followed the agricultural market. The Panic of 1819 caused a drop in prices, and by the mid-1820s male slaves were selling for only 650 dollars, women for 500 dollars. The economy recovered, and prices spiked in the late 1830s, when prime male slaves sold for about 1,200 dollars in New Orleans. The Depression of 1837 began another downturn, and by 1843 average slave prices had declined to about 500 dollars.[33]

Sally's transfer from Anthony Williams to John Miller was a private sale and clearly occurred in New Orleans. Miller denied even being in Attakapas at the time when the prosecution alleged that Salomé Muller had been kidnapped and enslaved there. Miller's witnesses all indicated that he did not own property in Attakapas when the slave Sally came into his possession. Carlile Pollock testified that he was employed exclusively as Miller's notary and thus was in a position to know about Miller's land acquisitions. Pollock recalled that Miller did not purchase Attakapas real estate until 1837 or 1838. Joachim Kohn, who acted as Miller's factor in Attakapas, put the date at no earlier than 1834 or 1835, as did three other witnesses.[34] Although slightly disparate, all the accounts placed Miller's Attakapas interest *after* the period when Salomé Muller might have been there, sometime between 1818 and 1822. In addition, land records and directories show that Miller acquired land in the region no earlier than 1833.[35]

Campbell's Directory of 1854 proclaimed, "The planters of Louisiana and of the South in general, are regarded (justly, we think,) the most intelligent, liberal and courteous population of the country."[36] By 1833, John F. Miller had become one of them. As his New Orleans enterprises prospered, Miller began branching out into rural holdings. First, he purchased land on

Butte à Peigneur (or Pine Island) in Lake Peigneur, eventually buying the entire island, which included a sugar plantation. He also began acquiring parcels of land in New Iberia, ultimately owning several thousand acres. There, along the Teche River, he started another sugar plantation. This one was especially large, and included a rum distillery, an overseer's house, and numerous slave cabins along the river. By 1838 he had built a large two-story brick home that became his and his mother's main residence, although they kept a house on Butte à Peigneur as well.[37]

Today St. Mary, Iberia, Vermilion, St. Martin, and Lafayette parishes form what was then known as the Attakapas region, and through it flows the Bayou Teche. The region was immortalized by Henry Wadsworth Longfellow, who called it the "Eden of Louisiana" in his poem "Evangeline." Settled by whites after 1810, the region, with alluvial soil from the river bottoms, boasted rich yields of cotton and sugar. But the land was wilderness, and the planters who settled the Attakapas prairie needed money to fund the clearing of land and building of levées. Establishing a sugar plantation was particularly capital-intensive. Because sugarcane rotted quickly once cut, most plantations processed the sugar on site. That meant buying and maintaining the necessary machinery. Several factors contributed to a growing interest in sugar cultivation in the 1820s: the introduction of a new cold-resistant cane, steam-powered equipment, and tariff protection. Although before 1830 Louisiana sugar was not highly sought after, Etienne Boré's successful efforts at producing granulation caused production to explode. Within two years, ten refineries had been established in Louisiana, and sugar soon became the Attakapas staple. Traveler Robert Baird, visiting the region in 1834, wrote that "the settlements in this state are totally dissimilar to those of any other state in our country, and are such as can hardly be conceived by those who have not seen them," adding that "nothing [could] exceed the beauty" of the riverfront plantations. He described them as extending along the river for a quarter to half a mile and then back from it a mile or more. The house was built along the river and, with slave quarters and mills, formed a "considerable village."[38]

The planter class represented what one scholar has termed a collection of "small, self-contained social orbits." In Attakapas, planters often met at each other's homes on Sundays for card parties and afternoon meals, while holidays and weddings gave particular cause for celebration. And of course, planter families frequently traveled to New Orleans for business, shopping, and entertainment. Once he joined this idle rich class, Miller began developing his Attakapas properties, especially Butte à Peigneur, into entertainment showplaces. He is credited with planting hundreds of orange trees there, giving it for a time the name "Orange Island." Miller also had a mile-long racetrack constructed on the island, and—along with David Weeks, owner of the neighboring plantation, Shadows-on-the-Teche—came to dominate racing in the region. With other prominent planters, Miller formed the Attakapas Jockey Club (or Turf Association) in 1835.[39]

In his involvement in horseracing, Miller was following a trend that was just beginning in the Crescent City area. Participation in sport was one of the many ways the upper class distanced itself from the masses, and horseracing was the first popular sport among the southern elite. They imported racing stock and organized jockey clubs to regulate racing and build grandstands. In southern Louisiana, sugar and cotton planters began organizing in the 1820s and 1830s. Several courses emerged, including those at St. Francisville, New Iberia, Alexandria, Donaldsonville, and Baton Rouge, with the biggest at Metairie in Jefferson Parish (today the site of Metairie Cemetery). Although racing attracted some support from all classes, most races were held on weekday afternoons, effectively precluding working-class attendance. Jockeys, however, came from the lower class, and in fact, many were slaves. Thus, horses, not their riders, were the focus of attention. Interest reached a peak in 1840 when 10,000 people attended New Orleans races. Area planters were intensely competitive, and by the 1850s, their efforts had paid off, when the racing newspaper *Spirit of the Times* judged New Orleans to be the national leader of thoroughbred racing.[40]

The lavish lifestyle of the Louisiana planter, however, was starting to fade for John Miller by the time of the trial. In February 1841, Miller found himself in court declaring bankruptcy. The details of his situation are not known but can be surmised. Miller lived well; one witness at the trial recalled that he "entertained much company at his house and drove the finest equipage in New Orleans." His ownership of several residences and businesses in New Orleans as well as the development and upkeep of two plantations indicated great wealth but also entailed great expense. Miller was not the first businessman to live beyond his means and fall into debt when the economy declined.[41]

In 1837 the nation suffered a severe economic depression. The preceding decades had seen intensely rapid business growth and when specie circulation could not keep pace with growth, people turned to credit. The nation expanded geographically, and markets became more interconnected. Overspeculation occurred—on cotton, land, banks, railroads, and canals—in a manner scholars have compared to that of the 1920s. Increasingly, doing business, especially on a large scale, became a gamble. The particular circumstances leading to the Panic of 1837 began in Britain. Two years of poor wheat harvests reduced incomes and textile demand, and in turn, British creditors pressed American debtors for payment and raised interest rates. Cotton prices, which had been rising steadily throughout the decade, now plummeted, and New Orleans merchants were hit first, beginning in March. Over the course of the year, virtually all the city's cotton factors were ruined. Sugar prices also dropped drastically and would remain low for years. The result was that Orleans Parish saw nearly three thousand lawsuits filed against debtors in 1837. The least diversified of all American cities, New Orleans had little manufacturing, relying heavily on cotton and commerce and, as such, was dependent on foreign trade and cotton sales to Britain. Moreover, rebuilding was hampered by nature. A flood in 1840 caused numerous crevasses (breaks) in the levée and destroyed cotton and sugar plantations.[42]

Miller, however, was more fortunate than many. By October 1842, he had been discharged from bankruptcy and returned to a decidedly comfortable, if not lavish, existence. He may have lost his New Orleans properties, but he retained his Attakapas plantations. His legal troubles, however, were far from over. When Sally first took her case to court, Miller had asked to be removed from warranty because he was bankrupt and claims against him were still pending. He was referring to a suit brought by his former factor Joachim Kohn, which was being appealed in the State Supreme Court, sitting at Opelousas in September 1843. Kohn had worked for Miller and Jonas Marsh, his partner in the New Iberia sugar plantation. Kohn argued that Miller and Marsh owed him for advances he had made them, including cash, clothing, and provisions, between January 1838 and August 1841, as well as a standard 10 percent annual interest on all advances. The District Court of St. Martin had awarded Kohn half the sum he claimed, and the Supreme Court affirmed the decision.[43]

It was about the time when Miller was experiencing financial problems that his sale of Sally to Louis Belmonti occurred. And it was the nature of her sale from Miller to Belmonti that produced the most damning allegation of the trial. Several witnesses had already claimed to recognize Sally as the missing Salomé. The evidence of her birthmarks was especially persuasive. Then Eve Schuber told the Court that, in the course of Sally's sale, John Miller had informed Louis Belmonti that his slave was in fact a white woman.

CHAPTER 6

Sally and Louis Belmonti

$\Longrightarrow$

*I*n the summer of 1838, John Miller sold Sally to Louis Belmonti, his neighbor in the Faubourg Marigny. Belmonti owned a grocery store at the corner of Piety and Levée streets. By 1841 he had moved to another location a block away, where the following year he opened a coffee house.[1] It was here that Madame Karl had discovered Sally. The business was variously described during the trial as a coffee house, a café, or a cabaret. The terms had different connotations. According to author Henry Castellanos, cabarets were public houses of entertainment that were "a great eyesore and a serious danger to the peace and good order of society." Found in markets and "other such places where negroes were wont to congregate," cabarets sold food and alcohol and sometimes provided a setting for gambling and the fencing of stolen goods. Castellanos quotes a contemporary, who declared such places "fruitful nurseries of vice and crime." More respectable establishments were known as coffee houses, although they usually served liquor as well. Men frequently transacted business at coffee houses like the one Benjamin Latrobe's son John visited in 1834. He described the New Exchange (or French) Coffee House, in the heart of the French Quarter, as a large room with columns and chandeliers, which "has always a crowd of frequenters who lounge and get and relate the news, and comprising people from every quarter of the globe who are gathered together in the commercial bustle of a great mart." Many of these establishments were open for business on Sundays.[2]

The location of such a business made a difference, too. What was described as a café in the downtown shopping mecca of Chartres Street or the prosperous middle-class American sector might have been a respectable shop. The location of Belmonti's establishments on the riverfront, however, where working people of all sorts, especially sailors, congregated, suggest something less elegant. And the Faubourg Marigny, downriver from the French Quarter, was decidedly working class. The district had once been the site of a plantation owned by wealthy Creole Bernard Marigny. Two developers approached him with grandiose plans to transform his land into the city's commercial center, the river being deep enough there to build docks. Marigny at first agreed but then backed out, developing the land on his own, although along the lines of their plan. But his dreams of grandeur were never realized. Americans and their capital were drawn to the Faubourg St. Mary, leaving the Faubourg Marigny to its poorer French, Spanish, and Creole inhabitants.[3] By 1840 free women of color owned 40 percent of the property there, a reflection of the plaçage system in which wealthy white men made formal arrangements with women of mixed race, sometimes living with them and their shared children.[4]

The pace of change in the Faubourg Marigny was slow. Historian Joseph Tregle, Jr., described it as "unkempt and sluggish," noting that it "lagged behind the rest of the city in almost every respect." Bishop Henry Whipple described the people of the Faubourg Marigny and Vieux Carré as living as their parents did, an indication that they lacked the "go-ahead" energy of the Yankees in the burgeoning Faubourg St. Mary. By 1836 there was such a marked division in New Orleans neighborhoods that the City Council created three municipalities, what Dennis Rousey calls "a partitioned urban government that was without parallel in nineteenth-century America." With the division, the economic differences grew more pronounced. The American sector prospered, boasting better transportation, wharves, a public school, a firehouse, and a municipal hall, while the French Quarter and the Faubourg Marigny languished. Canal Street became known as the Rubicon—a boundary that, once crossed, committed one forever. Bishop Whipple likened the municipalities to three different countries.[5]

Sally had been working in Louis Belmonti's Faubourg Marigny café for six years when she commenced her lawsuit. *How* she became Belmonti's slave is clear, although exactly *why* is not. The sale contract shows that on July 9, 1838, Belmonti purchased the slave Sally (called Mary in the document) from John F. Miller for seven hundred dollars. With Sally living and working at the house near Miller's sawmill, Belmonti likely had encountered her in the neighborhood. According to a Mr. A. Piernas, who acted as the broker in the sale, Belmonti had commissioned him to see if Miller would sell her. Piernas added that "she did not look like a colored person."[6]

Castellanos claimed that cabarets were owned mainly by foreigners "of a low class, chiefly Catalans, whose predilection for negro concubines was scandalous." Ethnic slurs aside, there is some evidence that Belmonti and Sally had had a prior relationship at the time he purchased her and that that relationship had been a sexual one. The bill of sale for Sally stipulates

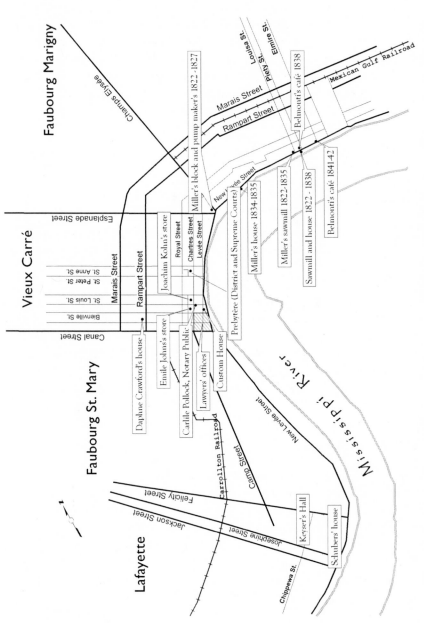

FIGURE 7. Map of New Orleans, based on Colton map of 1856, by Wendy Miller and students of the Washington College GIS Laboratory.

that, while her four-year-old son Charles was to remain under her care until the age of ten, he was still John Miller's property. Miller agreed to pay Charles's health expenses, but Belmonti assumed all other responsibility for his upkeep. Would he have agreed to do this unless the child was his? Miller's mother, Sarah Canby, said that Sally had told her Charles's father "was a frenchman, a shopkeeper who resided near us." Belmonti's name and the location of his business in the Faubourg Marigny suggest his French origins, as does the fact that the bill of sale for Sally is in French.[7]

By the time of Sally's sale in 1838, Miller had acquired two plantations in the Attakapas region, some one hundred miles from New Orleans. Since Belmonti had apparently initiated the purchase, it seems likely that he feared Sally's removal and, perhaps more importantly, his son's from New Orleans or at least the Faubourg Marigny and that he had orchestrated the sale to keep the two close to him. Further evidence from Sarah Canby depicts a relationship between Belmonti and Sally atypical of a master and a slave. Canby recalled that Sally and Belmonti came to visit some of her "servants" on Butte à Peigneur for several weeks in about 1843. Sally had also attended her own oldest son Lafayette's funeral there in 1839 and had stayed to visit.[8] Such freedom of movement was unusual for a slave and suggests the possibility that Belmonti allowed Sally to live as a free woman.

After being reunited with the woman she believed to be the missing Salomé Muller, Eve Schuber confronted Louis Belmonti with the facts of his slave's true identity as a white person. According to Schuber, Belmonti confessed that he had wanted to set Sally free, but Miller had told him that if she were freed, she would be forced to leave the country. Like many southern states, Louisiana had passed a law in 1830 requiring any manumitted slaves to leave the state within thirty days. Such laws were designed to reduce the number of manumissions and prevent the growth of a free black population that whites increasingly feared.[9] Belmonti told Miller, "But I have paid you my money for her." According to Belmonti, Miller replied either, "I did not sell her to you as a slave. She is a white woman and may go where she pleases," or "She is as white as you or I. And neither of us can hold her if she chooses to go away."[10] Interestingly, the 1840 census lists only one other resident at Belmonti's abode—under the category of "free colored female, age 24–36."[11]

In addition to Schuber's claim that both of Sally's owners knew she was white, the trial brought forth other witnesses who testified to Sally's ability to speak German, even more persuasive evidence that she was in fact Salomé Muller. A former employee at Miller's sawmill, A. M. Woods, recalled hearing Sally speak German back in 1821 or 1822. He was told by Mrs. Canby that the girl's father was dead and that she had been taken in as a charity case. Eventually, he said, it was hinted to him that he was becoming too "familiar" with Sally and he was told to leave. Another witness, Madame Poigneau, described as a Creole, recalled seeing the plaintiff as a young girl working at Miller's. She also remembered the girl speaking German. Poigneau was not the most effective witness. She was unable to tell the name of the street where she lived when she first met the plaintiff or even her own age. She said she had rarely spoken with the plaintiff, although she recalled the girl speaking German and having a German accent. Poigneau herself could no longer speak German, having forgotten it.[12]

Miller's witnesses countered that the plaintiff spoke neither German nor English with a German accent while she was Miller's slave.[13] They also indicated that many German immigrants were living and working in the vicinity of Miller's sawmill at the time of Salomé Muller's arrival, and had she been enslaved there, one of her compatriots surely would have noticed her. Two of the witnesses, Joachim Kohn and Emile Johns, were themselves immigrants. The German Kohn frequently saw the slave Sally when she came into his Chartres Street dry-goods shop with Mrs. Canby.[14] He described her speaking as "generally servants speak." Emile Johns, a composer and pianist, was born in Poland and educated in Vienna and had emigrated to New Orleans by early 1819. He had established a stationery store and a music printing business in the same block as Kohn's store.[15] Their shops were located at the west end of Chartres Street, where it connected with Canal Street, an area considered to be the "Broadway" of New Orleans because of its fine clothing, perfumes, and jewelry. Johns was familiar with the legal system, having won in 1841 the contract for printing the case reports (opinions of appellate judges) written by Merritt Robinson. The year before, he had also begun serving as the printer for Judah Benjamin's and Thomas Slidell's *Digest*.[16] Johns reported that he had visited Miller's mill nearly every day and had seen Sally yet had noticed no accent in her speech. He stated that, had there been a German girl there, he would have known it. W. Johnson, a ship's carpenter, knew Miller and his slave when he had worked in the navy yard and carried orders of timber from Miller's sawmill. He recounted that Sally had spoken English fluently and, more specifically, remembered her telling him she came from Mobile with Mr. Williams, who had sold her to Miller.[17]

People's impressions of Sally's speech were necessarily subjective. But Miller's witnesses raised an even more problematic issue for the prosecution. The slave Sally had given birth to a child in about 1825, when

Salomé Muller would have been, by her supporters' accounts, about ten years old. All of her witnesses had placed her age at the time of the 1818 journey to America at either three or four. That would have made her ten or eleven at the time of the baby's birth, not an absolute impossibility, perhaps, but extremely unlikely. By contrast, the slave Sally, according to the bill of sale and witnesses' accounts, was about fifteen years old when she became a mother—young but not impossibly so. Two of the defense witnesses dated the birth of Sally's baby from General Lafayette's visit to New Orleans in April 1825.[18] The general's visit was part of a tour of the United States honoring him for his role in the American Revolution. Congress had granted him 2 million acres of public land, which he chose in Florida, as well as a cash gift of two hundred thousand dollars. He received a positive reception throughout the nation, but in formerly French Louisiana, residents were absolutely captivated by his visit. Sally was not alone in naming her newborn boy after Lafayette.[19]

One exhibit presented in evidence by the defendant, however, actually contradicted his witnesses' claims about the infant's date of birth. In February 1823, less than a year after he had acquired her from Anthony Williams, Miller sold the slave then known as Bridget to his mother, Mrs. Sarah Canby, for the sum of 350 dollars. In December 1834, Canby sold Bridget, who by that time had three children—listed as Lafayette, age five, Madison, age three, and Adeline, age fifteen months—back to Miller for 350 dollars.[20] If Lafayette's age on this document is correct, he was born in 1829. Salomé Muller would have been fourteen that year, young for motherhood but not unimaginable.

In the 1834 sale contract, Bridget and her children are all identified as "mulatto." Who fathered her children? Miscegenation was illegal throughout the slave states and was not acknowledged in white southern society. Nevertheless, the population of mixed-race individuals in the slave and free black communities revealed that the practice did occur, usually in the form of masters' sexual exploitation of their female slaves. Slave narratives show, as John Blassingame puts it, "that many white men considered every slave cabin as a house of ill fame." While such behavior could be found everywhere, New Orleans was a city particularly known for its almost open acceptance of relationships between white men and black women.[21] Sally was a child of twelve when Miller acquired her, but sexual abuse of young girls was not unknown. She was light-skinned, and light-skinned slave women were valued for their beauty. And John Miller never married.

Eighteenth- and nineteenth-century observers commented on the frequency of interracial cohabitation in Louisiana and provided several explanations for its existence. It was suggested that white men were depraved and black women attractive and lusty. In an 1851 decision, the State Supreme Court explained that Spanish law had encouraged racial mixing by prohibiting provincial governors from marrying and by authorizing the keeping of mistresses. In actuality, the behavior arose from the particular demographic characteristics of the state's population. There were few white women in the colony; and that imbalance continued into the nineteenth century, although it declined somewhat over time. In 1840, white New Orleans had a surplus of more than 10,000 men. At no time before the Civil War did Louisiana have a balanced sex ratio in the white population. The inevitable result was that many white men began relationships with women of color, especially female slaves who were easily exploited. According to historian Richard Wade, "in New Orleans interracial relations became so common that a public tolerance if not acceptance grew up." Some scholars have suggested a cultural difference, finding French and Spanish attitudes more tolerant of miscegenation. But similar behavior among English colonists in the Caribbean suggests that demographics were more relevant than beliefs.[22]

Nowhere in any of the trial records is the possibility of a sexual relationship between John Miller and his slave Sally raised. Given that Sally's lawyers were trying any strategy to expose Miller as a criminal for holding a white woman in slavery, they likely would have mentioned sexual abuse had it occurred or been alleged. Some of Miller's own witnesses were very frank and gave damning testimony against him, yet none of them mentioned a sexual relationship between the two. The picture painted by witnesses also depicted Sarah Canby, not her son, as Sally's real owner in terms of daily contact.

Some explanation for the patrimony of Sally's children was provided at the trial. Several of the witnesses described her as "living with" another of Miller's slaves, a worker at the sawmill named Jim. He was identified as the children's father, and he and Sally had lived together and were considered to be married. Interestingly, Jim was described as being "as white as" Sally. Rosalie Labarre, whose husband kept a cabaret at Miller's mill, named Jim as the father of Sally's first child. Labarre stated that she was the child's godmother. Jonathan L. Lewis also testified that by November 1824 Sally was living with "one of Miller's colored boys, Jim, and was in the family way," thus dating her pregnancy even earlier than the other defense witnesses. Lewis described Jim, who was also known as "Yellow Jim," as looking as white as Sally.[23]

Slaves could not legally marry because the creation of a contract could have interfered with the master's right of ownership. Yet slave men and women nonetheless created a social institution of marriage that carried weight and meaning in their own community, if not that of whites. Most slave marriages were preceded by some kind of courtship, although time was obviously limited by slaves' work duties and sometimes owners' interference. Most marriages also involved a ceremony witnessed by the community, often presided over by a slave minister or the master. Many slave owners saw stable slave families as a factor that encouraged discipline and discouraged running away. Some sought to control their slaves' relationships, but slaves fought this intrusion as much as possible, sometimes simply disregarding the master's desire. Sarah Canby testified that Sally had asked her permission to marry fellow slave "Yellow Jim." When Canby refused, saying that Sally was not good enough for him, the two ignored Canby, and Sally was soon pregnant with Lafayette.[24] Many scholars note that young slave women had more autonomy to choose partners and to begin sexual relations than white girls did. Slave women bore their first child, on average, at about age twenty.[25]

For modern readers, all the previously discussed trial evidence might seem irrelevant. If Sally were actually a white person of exclusively European ancestry, would that not be obvious from her physical appearance? And wasn't the entire system of slavery based on clear racial distinctions? If only black people could be slaves and white people could not, surely there was some method of telling the two apart. But in the nineteenth century, as is still the case today, there existed a significant population composed of individuals who were both white and black—people of mixed race. How they fit into the social hierarchy was complicated. People of mixed racial background who were not slaves were designated "free people of color" and under southern states' laws often possessed special status. But what about people of mixed racial background who were slaves? While racial mixing was illegal in all southern states, it was also common, especially in Louisiana. One of the features of the *Miller v. Belmonti* trial was the minimal reaction that white witnesses had toward enslaved people who looked white.

In 1846, the *Daily Picayune*, for example, published two separate runaway slave notices describing white-looking slaves. One runaway was described as being "of a very clear color" with "sandy hair," and readers were warned that he might "try to pass himself for a white man." Another was described simply as a "white negro," with "blue eyes" and "very fair skin." Visitors to the city also commented upon the appearance of "white slaves." Charles Mackay visited a slave trader's establishment in New Orleans and encountered a man, "apparently white . . . with an unmistakable brogue." When questioned by Mackay, the man stated that his father was in fact Irish, but the dealer explained that the slave's mother had been a black slave, adding that he sometimes had for sale "much whiter men." Bishop Whipple, visiting the city in 1844, found at his boarding house a boy "as white as 9/10 of the boys at the north" yet a slave. Alexander Mackay, a British lawyer who saw New Orleans while on a tour of the United States in 1846–47, commented on the great degree of racial mixing. He described the city as having "five distinct bases" of population composition: Anglo-American, French, Spanish, African, and Indian, and added that, "not only is each of these to be found in it unmixed with any other, but they are all commingled, the one with the other, in a variety of ways and interminable degrees." Mackay added, however, that he believed that even when people of African descent had very light skin, some trace of their features marked them as African.[26]

The kind of caveat that accompanied Mackay's observation was also found in the testimony of some of the defense witnesses. Despite Sally's light complexion, John Miller's supporters argued that there was no question that she was anything other than a slave of African background. Several witnesses mentioned the fact that there were many mulattoes in the slave population and that light-skinned slaves were nothing out of the ordinary. Most witnesses referred to Sally as a quadroon, a legal designation that referred to a person of one-quarter black and three-quarters white ancestry, but was used more generally by the population to mean a light-skinned person of color. Defense witness W. Johnson testified that Sally "looked very fair" but was unsure whether she was a quadroon or white. Nathan Wheeler, John Miller's brother-in-law, recalled being struck by Sally's white complexion. He asked Miller if she was white and was told rather that she was a quadroon, but that she appeared so white that Miller was having trouble trying to sell her. Notary Carlile Pollock stated candidly that there were "many white persons of dark complexion and many colored persons of bright complexion," and added that there were "many colored persons in New Orleans who look like white families." Yet, he argued, it was possible to tell white from black because people living in an area populated by different races "acquire an instinctive means of judging that cannot be well explained."[27]

Jonathan L. Lewis provided even more compelling testimony on the question of Sally's racial background. Lewis had come to the city in 1803 from Kentucky when his father was appointed Territorial Supreme Court judge. At the time of the trial he was serving as major general of the first

FIGURE 8. Jonathan Lawson Lewis, carte de visite by A. Constant, ca. 1865. *Collection of the Louisiana State Museum.*

division of the Louisiana militia. He had previously worked as the clerk of the First District Court and would go on to serve as sheriff of New Orleans Parish and win election to the State Senate. In 1854, he became the "universally popular" (according to *Cohen's Directory*) mayor of New Orleans.[28]

In his testimony Lewis made two points. He noted that Sally had borne a child by another of Miller's slaves and stated emphatically that, if she had been white, this relationship would "not have been permitted." Lewis's comment implies, of course, that had people *known* Sally to be white, they would have prevented her interaction with a nonwhite man. But surely if people knew her to be white, she would not have been held illegally in slavery! Lewis then made the provocative statement that he perhaps had only assumed Sally was a slave because he saw her treated as such. He added that her skin color was "as white as most persons but he had seen slaves of as bright a color." Recalled to the stand later in the trial, Lewis expanded on his remarks, saying that he now saw a resemblance between Sally and one of her relations present in court (he referred probably to Eve Schuber). He said he had always believed Sally to be colored but now admitted that his belief "may have been induced by that fact that he had always seen her associating with persons of color." Similarly, another of Miller's witnesses, former employee H. B. Stringer, recalled of Miller's slave that "her light color excited his sympathy." He told the Court that "he took her to be very light, but her situation made him believe she was colored." [29]

Witnesses' assessments, then, were not definitive on the subject of Sally's appearance. Nor was there agreement on the other main points raised in the trial: whether Sally had ever spoken German, what her exact age was, and whether her origins could be proven as distinct from those of Salomé Muller's. With the trial still in progress, John F. Miller felt compelled to bring his version of events to a larger audience. On May 31 his letter, published in the *Daily Picayune*, reiterated his claim that Sally was nothing more than a slave and always had been. Miller's motivation was clear: he sought to restore his reputation and appears especially to have been responding to several earlier *Picayune* reports that were somewhat favorable to Sally. Having said his piece, Miller declared that he was willing to accept the judgment of the Court.[30]

CHAPTER 7

From Black to White

⹎

On June 25, 1844, a verdict was issued in favor of the defendants Louis Belmonti and John F. Miller. Presiding judge Alexander M. Buchanan explained the points he considered relevant in concluding that Sally was in fact a slave.[1] While he conceded that a little German girl named Salomé Muller had arrived in New Orleans in 1818 with her family and had become a redemptioner outside the city, he did not believe the prosecution had shown that the lost girl and the plaintiff were one and the same.[2]

Buchanan gave several reasons for his decision. First, the judge noted that the age of the plaintiff and the age of the lost German girl did not coincide. The slave Sally had given birth to a child in 1825 when Salomé would have been only ten years old. Second, the plaintiff had given an account of her origins different from the story told by the German witnesses. Here he referred to Sally's recollection of traveling across a big lake to New Orleans and of having Indian blood. Third, according to defense witnesses, when Miller acquired her in 1822, Sally had no trace of a German accent or appearance. In addition, Buchanan argued that the defense witnesses were more credible than those of the plaintiff. Virtually all of Sally's witnesses were German immigrants who had known Salomé Muller only as a child, some twenty-five years ago. Last, and possibly most important, the prosecution had not established a connection between John F. Miller and Salomé Muller. There simply was no evidence indicating that Miller had contracted for the labor of the Muller family in 1818. The record showed that Sally had come into his possession in 1822, no earlier. If the plaintiff was the real Salomé Muller, she had not managed to establish the link between her family's experience as redemptioners and John Miller's purchase of her as a slave in 1822.[3]

In a curious coda, Judge Buchanan suggested that if her supporters were still convinced that the plaintiff really was Salomé Muller, they could purchase her, adding that "they would doubtless find [the defendant] well disposed to part on reasonable terms, with a slave from whom he can scarcely expect any service, after what has passed."[4] Was this last statement an indication that the judge entertained some doubt about Sally's status? On each point where the plaintiff's and defendant's witnesses disagreed, Buchanan had sided with the defense. Yet his final comment hardly encouraged the retention of Sally in slavery. Perhaps he suspected she actually was who she claimed to be but found it difficult to side publicly with an enslaved woman against a prominent white businessman. Or he may have simply believed he was offering a practical solution.

Instead of following the judge's advice, however, Sally's lawyers lodged an appeal with the State Supreme Court just days after the District Court verdict. Sally's lawyer, Wheelock Upton, argued for a new trial on the grounds that the judgment was contrary to the evidence presented and that important new evidence had been uncovered recently.[5] Normally the introduction of new information was not permissible in a Supreme Court case, but freedom suits were an exception. The precedent was established in *Marie Louise v. Marot* (1835), in which Chief Justice George Mathews wrote that the Court was obliged to do everything possible to establish a plaintiff's claim of freedom, including consider new evidence.[6]

The additional testimony in this trial was significant indeed. Several new witnesses came forward to say that Sally's European ancestry had been known to John Miller before the trial. Eve Schuber had testified in the first trial that Sally's current owner, Louis Belmonti, had admitted that he knew his slave was a white woman. He claimed to have been told by her former owner that "I did not sell her to you as a slave. She is a white woman and may go where she pleases." Apparently Schuber's statement had not convinced Judge Buchanan, but now Upton provided corroborating testimony from Peter Curren, a pilot at the Balize, who knew Belmonti and had frequently discussed the trial with him. Curren claimed that Belmonti told him that, just a few weeks after his purchase of Sally, he quarreled with her and went to Miller to try to rescind the sale. Miller then told him that she was in fact white and had "all the rights of a free white person, and was only to be held as a slave by kindness and coaxing." Belmonti told Curren that he had been so angry upon hearing this that he had wanted to shoot Miller. When the freedom suit was initiated, Belmonti told Curren he had always feared something like that would happen.[7]

Upton's motion also offered the statement of an engineer named Fribee who, when employed by Miller, remembered the slave Sally speaking with a German accent. Fribee had not testified at the first trial because the prosecution did not know his whereabouts and had only recently discovered that he was working on a sugar plantation in Bayou Plaquemine. In addition, Nathan Wheeler, Miller's brother-in-law, who had testified in the first trial, had since remembered a mulatto girl named Bridget coming to Miller's around 1822. He described her as "very considerably darker in complexion than the Plaintiff" and said that she was no longer there after three or four years. He assumed that she had died. The implication was that it was actually she, and not Sally, who was the subject of the 1822 sale contract.[8]

Upton also recalled the testimony of Madame Bertrand, which had not become part of the record of the first trial. Unable for health reasons to attend court and testify in person, Bertrand was to be deposed by counsel for both sides, but some confusion over the meeting resulted in Upton's being the only one to arrive at her house. Without defense counsel present, no official statement was taken. Judge Buchanan had refused a continuance to resolve the situation. Upton argued that Bertrand's statement was crucial. She had been the midwife at the birth of Sally's first child, the only person present at that event other than Sally and Sarah Canby. Bertrand recalled that the birth had taken place in 1827 or 1828, several years after the defense's alleged date, placing Sally's age at the birth of her first child at seventeen or eighteen (based on her age as recorded in the 1822 sale contract).[9]

Upton now highlighted the defense's contradiction of its own documents with regard to the age discrepancy. The original bill of sale from Anthony Williams to Miller recorded "Bridget's" age as "about twelve" in 1822, putting the year of her birth at 1810. The record of Miller's sale of Sally to Belmonti lists her age in 1838 as twenty-two, putting her birthdate in 1816. Even more damning, the 1834 record of her sale from Miller to Canby lists the age of her child Lafayette as five, putting his birth in 1829, four years later than Miller had claimed in the trial. Upton informed the Court that he had sent a friend, a Mr. Eimer, who was traveling to visit his parents in Alsace, to obtain a copy of Salomé Muller's birth certificate. A handwritten note at the bottom of the page indicates that the certificate had arrived and "sets this all right—she was born in July 1813."[10]

This knowledge helped the prosecution's case in one way: a girl born in 1813 conceivably could have had a child by 1828 or 1829. Becoming a mother at age fifteen or sixteen was perhaps atypical but by no means medically impossible. But the information also threatened the case in another way. The birth certificate showed that several of the German witnesses had gotten Salomé's age wrong. Three witnesses accurately recalled her age as three or four; she was in fact three when the family left Alsace and four when they arrived in this country. But two witnesses—one of them Eve Schuber—remembered her as being just two years old.[11] Prosecution counsel did not really have to address the issue because the birth certificate spoke for itself, but the error could serve to reduce the credibility of the German witnesses. If their memories were wrong about this fact, what else were they remembering inaccurately? Fellow passengers might have mistaken Sally's age, thinking she was younger than she actually was. Perhaps she was small for her age as a result of malnutrition; starvation had been a problem on the voyage. But surely those family members close to her, as Eve Schuber claimed to be, would have known her real age.

Upton also raised the issue of the real Salomé Muller's whereabouts. Surely, he argued, if she were still alive and living in Attakapas or Opelousas, she would have appeared to set the record straight. "Has not this petition been the subject of conversation and newspaper comment in every Parish in the State?" he asked. Upton might have been exaggerating the publicity given to the case and the accessibility of news in the countryside distant from New Orleans, but his point was a fair one. Even Miller's defense witness William Turner had testified that the case "had been the talk of the town for some months." If Salomé Muller lived in another part of the state, surely she or someone else would have come forward with that information. Furthermore, John Miller and his mother owned two large plantations in Attakapas, where they were well known. With the resources available to them, surely they could have discovered the "real" Sally. The fact that they hadn't, Upton argued, implied that she really was the plaintiff.[12]

Upton alleged that Judge Buchanan had erred in claiming that Sally's supporters had seen in her merely a resemblance to the Muller family. He reminded the Court that several witnesses positively identified her as *the* Salomé Muller. Two of them were particularly in a position to know: Eve Schuber, her godmother, who had nursed her on the voyage, and her cousin Daniel Muller, who had known her since her birth. The German witnesses had also referred to the birthmarks on Sally's legs, which the examination of two doctors had shown to be present on the plaintiff from birth.[13]

Last, Upton raised the issue of race. He argued that the plaintiff did not have any African features in either her appearance or behavior (without identifying exactly what those features might have been). Moreover, the fact that she had won the friendship of so many whites was evidence of her being white. He noted: "The perseverance, the uniform good conduct, the quiet and constant industry, which are found in those she claims as relatives, have always been found in her, and however polluted and degraded her person may have been, these traits have yet left her worthy of the relatives who ask at your hands—*and these traits prove her white nature*" (emphasis original). The level of community support that Sally had garnered represented to Upton "an influence . . . no one but a white woman could possibly raise up and control." [14]

The case was not considered by the Court until June 1845. The Louisiana Supreme Court had been established by the Constitution of 1812, with the state divided into two judicial districts. The Eastern District seat was in New Orleans, the Western at Opelousas. A geographically spreading population soon sent the Court riding circuit to other towns as well, including Baton Rouge, Shreveport, Monroe, and Alexandria, during September and October. The Court met from November through July in New Orleans and then recessed for August. [15]

Four judges heard the appeal: François-Xavier Martin, Henry Adams Bullard, Edward Simon, and Rice Garland. The fifth, Alonzo Morphy, was absent due to illness. Martin was the senior judge and perhaps the most distinguished of the group. Born in Marseilles, he had come to the United States at the age of twenty, living first in North Carolina, where he worked as a printer and studied law. He was appointed to the Louisiana State Supreme Court in 1815 and served as chief justice from 1836 to 1846. In 1816, after the legislature authorized a compilation of the state's laws, Martin produced a three-volume work. He was also a serious historian. He served as the president of the Louisiana Historical Society and wrote a history of the state that is still well regarded by scholars. He died not long after the opinion was rendered in the *Miller v. Belmonti* case. [16]

Martin's appointment as chief judge coincided with, or possibly caused, the Court's entrance into a period of decline. A variety of issues had combined to seriously clog the dockets by the mid-1830s. In 1841, Gustavus Schmidt, editor of the short-lived *Louisiana Law Journal,* claimed that a petitioner might have to wait up to fourteen years for his or her case to be heard. Hyperbole or not, his allegation elucidated the fact that the Court was in need of serious reform. The Depression of 1837 had brought an enormous number of financial disputes onto the docket. And both George Mathews and Martin suffered from ill health. Some blamed the Court's backlog on François-Xavier Martin himself; for despite going blind, he would neither retire nor approve of reforms to accelerate the movement of cases. The judges heard arguments only five hours a day, three days a week, and often spent time talking rather than listening to lawyers. Louisiana Democrats, rewriting the state constitution, saw a chance to solve the problems that plagued the Court. Their reforms included term limits of eight years for judges and creation of an office of chief justice with explicit powers beyond simple deference to the Court's most senior judge. [17]

An earlier attack on Martin had involved John Miller's counsel, John Grymes. Grymes apparently had been one of the supporters of a legislative resolution to impeach Martin in 1819. The source of the complaint was a lawyer and legislator named Christobal De Armas. Records of the debate have not survived, but Henry A. Bullard described it in a letter written in 1822 while he was serving in the state legislature. Although the resolution accused Martin of forging a petition brought by De Armas to the Court to alter its meaning, Bullard wrote that he did not believe the allegation. He said, "The truth is that Martin has been extremely obnoxious here to a few that lead the flock—They call him renegade because he upholds the language of the Constitution; and will not tolerate the French language in Judicial proceedings." Although Martin was not impeached, De Armas and his supporters tried hard to remove him, and Grymes himself delivered "a most violent Philippic against the Judges." Historian Richard Kilbourne suggests that Grymes was motivated by his desire to retain connections to the French community and benefit from his knowledge of the dual system.[18]

Henry Adams Bullard, the author of the *Miller v. Belmonti* opinion, was no less accomplished than Martin but had had a more varied career. Born in Massachusetts in 1788, he was the son of a Presbyterian minister and a mother related to John Adams. Bullard graduated from Harvard, read law in Philadelphia, fought in the Mexican Revolution, and then settled in Nachitoches, where he married, fathered five children, and started a law practice. In 1822, he was elected to the Louisiana legislature and in 1830 to the U.S. Congress. Four years later he was appointed to the State Supreme Court. His term was briefly interrupted in 1839 when he was appointed secretary of state of Louisiana, but he resigned after less than a year when Chief Justice Martin declared that Bullard's place on the bench could not be filled. Bullard remained on the Court until 1846 when a new bench was formed. He returned to private practice and then served in the state legislature and the U.S. Congress. In his later years he also was a professor of civil law at the University of Louisiana. Like François-Xavier Martin, Bullard helped form the Louisiana Historical Society in 1835 and served as its president until his death in 1851. Like Martin, Bullard left his mark upon the state's legal history, co-authoring with Thomas Curry the 1842 revision of the legal code.[19]

Edward Simon, the least well known of the justices, left his native Belgium when he was eighteen. Emigrating first to London, he then took up the cotton business in Baltimore before moving to Louisiana. After retirement from the bench, he became a sugar planter. He was the first of four generations of Simons to serve on the State Supreme Court.[20]

The fourth member of the Court, Rice Garland, was the most notorious. Just months after hearing the *Miller v. Belmonti* appeal, he involved the Court in a highly publicized scandal. In October 1845, Garland was publicly accused of forging the signature of wealthy philanthropist John McDonough on a note for six thousand dollars. (The signature was apparently real but was affixed to a note of which McDonough had no knowledge.) When confronted, Garland begged McDonough to cover the note, which he did. On December 8, when Garland arrived to take his seat in court, Martin adjourned in protest; and he and his colleagues turned the matter over to the District Court. Garland tried to commit suicide by jumping off a steamboat into the Mississippi River but was rescued. He left for Texas in 1846 and practiced law there until his death in 1861.[21]

These, then, were the four men to decide Sally's fate. In summing up the Supreme Court's opinion, Bullard first addressed the issue of the plaintiff's physical appearance. He noted that the 1810 case of *Adelle v. Beauregard* had established the legal precedent that persons of color were presumed free, the burden of proof thus falling on the person who claimed someone as a slave. The opinion in that case, written by Martin, reasoned that people of color (meaning here persons of mixed race) could have been descended from Indians, one white parent, or free people of color.[22] The proof with regards to Sally's complexion, Bullard wrote, was strong. There was no evidence of her having African parentage, which was crucial to proving slave status. The members of the Court were particularly impressed by the testimony of Jonathan L. Lewis, who was referred to as "one of the most intelligent and candid witness on the part of the defendant." Lewis had indeed been candid, describing the slave Sally as looking "as white as most persons." He had also noticed her resemblance to members of the Muller family present in court. The judges apparently did not examine the plaintiff's appearance themselves.[23]

The defendants had argued that under Spanish law, when the master in a freedom suit produced title to the slave, the burden of proof then fell upon the plaintiff. The Digest of 1808 and the Civil Code of 1825 were designed to bring Louisiana law into line with that of other American states by removing its Roman, French, and Spanish heritage. But this heritage faded slowly, and judges and lawyers used it only when it served them. Historian Thomas Ingersoll argues that differences between American and French law caused less conflict than some have claimed. The law in Louisiana was what it was in the rest of the South—whatever the planter class said it was. In this instance, the Court focused on a different law, noting that seller Anthony Williams had authorized the sale of a child ("apparently white") at a time when the sale of *any* slave child from its mother was illegal.[24]

Bullard concluded that "if there be in truth two persons, about the same age, bearing a strong resemblance to the Millers [Mullers] and the plaintiff is not the real lost child . . . *it is certainly one of the most extraordinary things in history*" (emphasis in original). This time, the four sitting judges agreed with the plaintiff. The Supreme Court declared Sally Miller a free white woman and ordered her released from slavery.[25]

A party was held at Keyser's Hall in Lafayette, home of Sally and many of her German friends, to celebrate the victory. Keyser's (or Kaiser's) was the more sedate of two Lafayette ballrooms favored by Germans. It served many purposes: coffee house during the day, host to political meetings and social gatherings in the evenings. Keyser's hall was also the site of Catholic mass for about a year while a permanent church, St. Mary's, was being built. (Mass was held in German, French and English.)[26] According to one newspaper account, the celebration of Sally's freedom involved "music and dancing, a sumptuous feast and an abundance of rich wines, and they enjoyed themselves until a late hour. More than two hundred ladies were present—the rich, the beautiful, the accomplished representatives of the best portion of our German resident population." Sally's attorney, Wheelock Upton, was the subject of the first toast, and he replied with a lengthy speech in her honor. "When we consider her sex, her station, and her means," Upton told the crowd, "and contrast them with the wealth, and the power, and the influence of those who contended against her, it is indeed a matter of gratulation and joy that her success was triumphant. Truth, however mighty it may be in its simplicity, has not always prevailed against the machinations of the wicked and the arts of the fraudulent." Upton appealed to the German community to continue its support of Sally and acknowledged that, although her case was won, she still had to make her way in the world. He reached out to the women present, urging them not to hold Sally's past against her but to take her under their wing and, in essence, teach her how to be white. One newspaper found significance in the ballroom's decor: "The room was well adorned with the emblems of American liberty, and *that* 'Star-Spangled Banner' which has so long floated o'er *our* 'land of the free and home of the brave,' was the principal decoration of the room where this happy reunion took place" (emphasis in original).[27]

But the victory celebration proved to be premature. John Miller would not accept defeat at the hands of his former chattel. After losing his case in the Supreme Court, Miller retaliated against Sally, suing her for fraud. And this time, Miller alleged, he had discovered the *real* Salomé Muller.[28]

CHAPTER 8

White Slavery

⚜

$\mathcal{T}$he case of Sally Miller is a fascinating story of the life of one antebellum American slave woman. But it also provides a window through which to view a central tension in American history: the struggle to comprehend the concept of race. Sally Miller's life and legal challenge raise provocative questions about how definitions of race have been constructed and interpreted throughout American history. Could a white person have become enslaved in the antebellum United States, a society that pointedly equated slave status with black skin? Could a German immigrant have been mistaken for an African American? If Sally Miller the slave was also Salomé Muller the German immigrant, then *how* could a white person have been enslaved under a social and legal system that mandated slavery predicated on race? Nineteenth-century scholar of slave law Thomas R. R. Cobb articulated the prevalent American belief—simply, that "white persons may not be enslaved." Cobb also claimed (inaccurately) that, since all black people had been brought into the American colonies as slaves originally, it was logical to assume slave status from dark skin color.[1] For white southerners, this racial divide was not only a reality but a positive good. As the *Mobile Register* explained, for example, in 1859: "We can have a healthy State of society with but two classes—white and slave."[2] The categorization was clear, and whites took comfort in these neatly delineated boundaries. Of the slave states, only Delaware, with an antebellum black population comprised mainly of free people, did not codify presumption of slavery from skin color.[3]

But while slavery in the United States was *essentially* black slavery, it was not *exclusively* so. Colonial lawmakers decided early on that the most convenient method of determining racial status was to mandate that a child would inherit the condition of his or her mother.[4] Such laws had two advantages. Maternity was easily determined at the time of birth; paternity was not. And because the majority of mixed-race couplings in the country took place between slave women and white men (often their owners), maintenance of the slave labor force was supported by natural increase. Female offspring produced by such unions, however, were partially white, although slave, and when they in turn had children by white men, producing even whiter offspring, a slave population developed over time that was in both appearance and genetic background essentially white.

In some parts of the Americas, a complex social and legal hierarchy recognized the reality of racial mixing, but this was not the case in the colonies that became the United States. As Winthrop Jordan has noted, "From the first, every English continental colony lumped mulattoes with Negroes in their slave codes and in statutes governing the conduct of free Negroes." Identification was based not on genetic composition but on appearance: anyone who looked even slightly black was assigned black status. People who visibly appeared to be black were generally presumed to be slaves; beyond that, southern colonies did not immediately and systematically create legal definitions of race. But slavery was increasingly challenged after the Revolutionary War, and as the number of manumissions grew, it became both more necessary and more difficult to determine who could be enslaved. State legislatures began addressing the issue, creating formulas for determining race. Generally, a person with at least one-eighth black ancestry (that is, who had one black great-grandparent) was defined as black. The apparent genetic precision of such laws gave white southerners a sense of security. But with accurate genetic information frequently unavailable, physical appearance was often the more relevant factor in determining an individual's race.[5]

Scholars have documented that New Orleans was notable for its large mixed-race population, which was recognized as a distinct caste. John Blassingame has called racial mixing "the most unique feature of race relations in antebellum New Orleans." Referring to an 1850 advertisement in which an owner suggested that his slave might attempt to pass for white, Judith Kelleher Schafer notes that "Passing for white in New Orleans, with its olive-skinned whites of French and Spanish ancestry, would be easier than in most southern cities." Thomas Ingersoll argues that antebellum free blacks, a largely mixed-race group, remained isolated as a community because of their intermediate status. Because they reproduced within this closed community, he notes, "by the 1860's New Orleans had a remarkably white population of 'free blacks' that surprised all outsiders."[6]

Nor were such cases restricted to the city. Solomon Northup, the kidnapped New Yorker who wrote an account of his twelve years enslaved in rural Louisiana, recalled a white-looking slave he knew on a sugar plantation in Bayou Boeuf. Celeste, age nineteen, was described as looking "far whiter than her owner, or any of his offspring." Northup added: "It required a close inspection to distinguish in her features the slightest trace of African blood. A stranger would never have dreamed that she was the descendant of slaves."[7]

The state of Louisiana was also somewhat unusual in its generosity toward defining mulatto status. In Sally Miller's Supreme Court appeal, Judge Henry Adams Bullard explained that, under Louisiana law, a person of color (in nineteenth-century legal terms, a person of mixed racial background) was presumed free; therefore, the burden of proof fell upon the person claiming another as his or her slave. Citing the argument from *Adelle v. Beauregard* (1810), Bullard wrote, "Persons of color may have descended from Indians on both sides, from a white parent, or mulatto parents in possession of their freedom. Considering how much probability there is in favor of the liberty of these persons, they ought not to be deprived of it upon new presumptions, most especially as the right of holding them in slavery, if it exists, is in most instances, capable of being satisfactorily proven."[8] This presumption of freedom was especially applicable in the case of a person already living as free. Ownership, however, particularly when supported by written title, could be considered evidence of slave status, although not always conclusively so.[9]

The enslaving of mulattoes, especially those who were very light-skinned in appearance, made enslavement of whites a possibility. If only "full-blooded" Africans and their descendants had been enslaved, a white person held in bondage would have been instantly noticed. Why did whites create and perpetuate a system of racial designation that was arbitrarily enforced and, as a result, potentially placed whites themselves in jeopardy? Part of the answer lies in the fact that not all whites were equally at risk of becoming slaves. White men and women of the elite, and their successive generations of offspring, were able to protect themselves. Wealth, status, land ownership, and literacy all enabled an individual to prove his or her white identity. Land ownership encouraged a written record of the elite's material and economic ties; literacy made maintenance of the record possible. The attention that wealthy whites paid to their ancestry also made such challenges to their freedom unlikely. But for the impoverished, those who were illiterate and ignorant of the legal system, immigrants, and children, defending themselves against illegal enslavement was infinitely more difficult. And once an individual was claimed as a slave, the general presumption of slave status rendered assertions of freedom hard to sustain.

But southern whites accepted the discrepancy between reality and perception of racial slavery because it allowed them (at least those in power) to determine an individual's status. As Frederick Douglass noted, "I knew of blacks who were *not* slaves; I also knew of whites who were *not* slaveholders; and I knew of persons who were *nearly* white, who were slaves. *Color,* therefore, was a very unsatisfactory basis for slavery . . . nor was I long in finding out another important truth, viz: what man can make, man can unmake." [10] Sally Miller claimed that she had been transformed into a black person because John Miller said she was black; she then became white because the Louisiana Supreme Court decided she was white.

In the modern world, science has shown racial categorization to lack validity. Biologists have demonstrated the impossibility of assigning certain genetic traits to specific groups with any reliability: variance within groups is greater than the differences between groups. [11] This is the result of population interaction throughout human history, which has occurred much more frequently than early scholars or the general public have been willing to accept. In the United States, miscegenation among Europeans, Africans, and Native Americans happened during the groups' first encounters, and over time, an immense variety of genetic combinations was produced in successive generations. [12]

But whites in power, especially those who held slaves or traded them, possessed an obvious financial incentive to cling to racial, and racist, theories. For well-placed northern whites, peace and accommodation with their southern counterparts made any serious reconsideration of racial stereotypes politically and financially inconvenient. For poor whites, both southern and northern, the assurance of some "natural" and immutable distinction between them and anyone of African or Native American descent cushioned the plight of daily material deprivation. So, too, did nineteenth-century immigrant Americans, already held suspect because of their "foreign ways," find in race one means of status in the polyglot pecking order of New World life. In other words, almost every white had a self-interest in embracing race as a valid concept, to the detriment of all blacks and any whites who got caught on the wrong end of that either-or measuring rod. And because whiteness was ultimately impossible to *prove,* some whites did find themselves held as slaves. The fact that some mulattoes were very light-skinned in appearance, favoring their white parents or grandparents, accounts for many of the reports of "white" slaves. But evidence shows that there were others who were apparently wholly of European descent.

One example, the case of Mary Gilmore, aptly illustrates the social context of race. Abolitionist William Jay related Gilmore's story in his

readers in the distant North, observers of the case chose sides, all finding information to bolster their different positions. Each witness, each new piece of evidence that was introduced, pulled public opinion first in one direction and then in the other. Two stories were told in the courtroom: the tale of Salomé Muller, a little girl traveling to the New World with her family, and that of Sally (or Bridget or Mary), a lifelong slave of African descent. Whether they represented the stories of two different women or one and the same woman was a question that threatened both the Louisiana legal system and white southerners' notions of race.

CHAPTER 9

Sally Miller and Salomé Muller

＝✝

Sally's story did not end with the Lafayette celebration. Emboldened by victory, she and her supporters initiated efforts to win not only the hearts and minds of the citizens of New Orleans but substantial monetary damages as well. Two of her children, Madison and Adeline, also remained in Miller's possession, and she sought their return. (The eldest, Lafayette, had died; the youngest, Charles, was with her.) The Supreme Court had rendered its judgment on June 21, 1845. Four days later, Sally's legal team brought suit in Federal Court against John F. Miller and his mother, Sarah Canby. In the days between the ending of the one suit and the commencement of the other, a pamphlet appeared in New Orleans entitled "Sally Miller," providing the public with Sally's side of the story. Though published anonymously, the pamphlet was assumed by Miller to be the work of Wheelock Upton, and given the information contained therein and the style of writing, Upton's authorship does seem likely. A story in the *New Orleans Tropic* indicates that the pamphlet was published at the newspaper's office by one of Sally's attorneys.[1] The document, twenty-four pages long, contained an account of the life of Salomé Muller. It told of her origins in Alsace, her arrival in the United States, her discovery by the German community, and the lawsuit against her former owners Belmonti and Miller. Upton recounted the trial arguments and testimony in some detail, paying particular attention to the discrepancy in Sally's age in the various accounts given by Miller, his mother, and their supporters. He implies that the errors on the part of her former owners were in fact deliberate lies. He also refers to the new evidence uncovered after the judgment (that of Nathan Wheeler, Peter Curren, and Fribee the engineer), all of which furthered Sally's case when their testimony was submitted in the appeal.[2]

In addition, however, Upton also referred to evidence that did not find its way into the appeal:

> (It may be well to state here, that since the trial, and since the motion for a new trial, other witnesses of character, standing, and the utmost respectability have been discovered, who do not hesitate in their identification of the Plaintiff as the *same person whom they knew in the employment of John F. Miller in 1820, 1821 and 1822, who spoke very imperfect and broken English, and with an evident German accent—that she was then 8, 9, or 10 years of age—that she was a little white German girl, and was spoken of by Miller, his mother, and the household, as a little orphan girl whom he, Miller, had received from a ship, and that she had to work a certain time to pay her passage.*) [parentheses and emphasis in original]

Was Upton getting ahead of himself? Was he banking on evidence he had heard of but hadn't yet collected? Some trial witnesses did recall a little white-looking girl speaking with an accent at Miller's, but no one mentioned an orphan coming from a ship as an indentured servant. It is possible that this particular testimony is simply missing from the trial transcript. It is not referred to elsewhere and was reprinted in neither Upton's pamphlet nor Miller's rebuttal, both of which extensively recounted the original trial testimony. Even here Upton is curiously vague. He mentions the testimony of Wheeler, Curren, and Fribee specifically but refers to no other witnesses. The pamphlet closes with the Supreme Court's judgment declaring Sally Miller a free white woman.[3]

While the pamphlet sought to win public support, the way to win financial settlement and the return of Sally's children was through the legal system. Bypassing the District Court this time, Upton filed suit on behalf of his client in the U.S. Circuit Court, Fifth District of Louisiana, sitting in New Orleans. Perhaps he sought to avoid a second encounter with Judge Buchanan, who had ruled against Sally originally. Perhaps, too, he hoped for a better reception from a jury rather than a judge. (One of the distinctive features of the Louisiana legal system was the preponderance of bench trials without a jury.)[4] In the petition, filed exactly a year to the day after the District Court verdict declaring her to be a slave, the plaintiff claimed that when

> yet of tender age and too young either to assert or to be aware of her rights, she was illegally and feloniously seized by one John F. Miller

and . . . Sarah Canby, your petitioner was converted and raised as a slave—her natural liberty debarred her, she was made to hold a place with negroes and those born to servitude, severe tasks and burdens were imposed upon her, cruel and wicked punishments were inflicted, ranked with slaves treated as a slave and taught only the duties of a slave your petitioner did for more than twenty years suffer the hardships and privations imposed upon her by the African race.[5]

Sally asked the Court for two things. First, she wanted the return of her children, Madison and Adeline, now adolescents, who were still in the possession of Miller and Canby. Her claim to free status having been proven in the State Supreme Court, her children should be legally free as well because a child's status followed the mother's condition of servitude. Second, she asked the Court to compensate her for more than twenty years in illegal bondage: twenty thousand dollars for her labor, fifty thousand for her pain and suffering, five thousand for the pain and suffering of her children, and however much more a jury might be willing to award.[6]

While the dollar amounts seem high, seventy-five thousand dollars may not be outrageous for nearly a quarter-century of illegal enslavement. John F. Miller was a wealthy businessman and planter who stood accused of holding a white woman in bondage. Sally was perhaps not naïve to believe she could obtain at least some compensation for the wrong done to her. And her demand for return of her children is unquestionably reasonable. There was no justification for holding them in slavery once their mother's status as a white person had been legally established. Adeline was of mixed race, her father a slave of African descent, while Madison's father was a white man.[7] But in determining the legal status of slaves, only the mother's condition was relevant. Slave women gave birth to slave children; free women bore free children, regardless of paternity.

The response of the defendants Miller and Canby was to be expected: they denied Sally's claim that she was in fact a white woman born in Germany.[8] But more significant was a series of depositions collected by Commissioner Copeland Hunt in December 1845 and January 1846 from a group of people in the northeastern part of Louisiana who told a story of Salomé Muller very different from the one previously heard. The Supreme Court had concluded that "if there be in truth two persons, about the same age, bearing a strong resemblance to the Millers [Mullers] and the plaintiff is not the real lost child . . . *it is certainly one of the most extraordinary things in history*" [emphasis in original].[9] John Miller disagreed; and he

had been busy working to show that the Court had erred, that the extraordinary was in fact true, and that there were two Salomé Mullers—one genuine, the other a fraud.

Officials began taking depositions in the Circuit Court case in
December, but much of the information that would appear in the witnesses'
statements was already being made public in New Orleans. In December
1845, Miller had published his own pamphlet rebutting the allegations contained in Upton's pamphlet. Like Upton, Miller reprinted much of the trial
testimony, but not before treating his readers to nearly twenty pages of vit-
riol directed at his former chattel and her legal counsel. Miller makes clear
his intent from the start: "For the value of the slave, I care nothing. . . . I do
care for my reputation and the reputation of a mother now ninety years old."
The Court's decision had not left him chastened: "Counsel, witnesses, and
client, they were all worthy of each other, and I defy and despise them all." [10]

Miller questioned the accuracy of the memories of many of Sally's
German supporters, who claimed to recall her when she was a little girl,
more than twenty years ago. He provided two explanations for their behavior. One was the possibility of securing monetary rewards and notoriety.
Miller is not more specific, but presumably he suggests that some witnesses
expected to share in the funds gained in the suit for damages. Others may
have enjoyed being part of an event attracting attention around the city.
Miller's mother, who provided her own statement in the pamphlet, charged
that Sally was the "dupe" of others who were desirous of "extorting money,
and forcing themselves into public notice, for their own advancement and
notoriety." [11]

The other explanation Miller offered was the influence of group
behavior. He argued that surely some of the many Germans who had come
to the city with the Muller family in 1818 had encountered his slave moving about the city on her daily errands. Yet until Madame Karl's discovery
of her at Belmonti's café in 1843, none had ever come forward. Then, suddenly, numerous relations and compatriots recognized her. Miller argued
that they "no doubt were unwilling to be thought inferior to Madame Carl
[*sic*], in seeing, believing, remembering, swearing, or anything else." [12]

Miller also pointed out the selective nature of the German witnesses'
memories. For example, they swore they recalled the birthmarks on her
thighs, yet none correctly remembered Salomé's age at the time of the voyage. As her birth certificate showed, she was nearly five when she came to
this country, easily old enough to retain some memory of her circumstances
at the time and over the next few years. Yet she apparently held no memory

of any of it whatsoever and for the next quarter-century apparently never said a word to anyone even hinting at her true identity. The German witnesses took pains to establish their respectability as middle class, but the wealthy Miller clearly looked down on them as working class, as well as foreigners, calling them "Low Dutch." [13]

But Miller directed his greatest hostility at a member of his own family. Nathan Wheeler was married to Miller's younger sister, Mary Ann. Wheeler had testified in the first trial that Sally's son Lafayette had been born in 1825 or 1826, helping to establish the fact that she was too old to be Salomé Muller. [14] After the trial concluded, though, he decided that he had been mistaken—that the child had actually been born two years later, in 1827 or 1828. Upton used this new testimony in the petition for a new trial. [15] Wheeler had not merely changed his mind, Miller argued, but had deliberately falsified his statement to seek revenge on his brother-in-law. Wheeler and his family, according to Miller, had "long lived on my charity, and when it was no longer in my power, owing to the loss of my fortune, to contribute to their support as liberally as in former days, he basely deserted his wife and child, who are thus thrown on me for their daily bread." Miller added that he had produced Lafayette's baptismal certificate, which proved that he was born in 1825. [16]

Sarah Canby saved her venom for Sally, treating readers to an account of her former slave's sexual history. She stated that, about two years after coming into Canby's possession, Sally asked permission to marry Yellow Jim, another of Miller's and Canby's slaves. Canby refused because, she wrote, "even at that early age she [Sally] was an abandoned character, and gave me a great deal of trouble." Nonetheless, by the end of the year, Sally and Jim were the parents of a child, named Lafayette after the visiting French patriot. Four years later, another son was born to Sally, this one named Madison and, according to Canby, fathered not by Jim but by a white man named Struve who worked for Miller. Next was Adeline, fathered by Jim Bigger, another slave, who worked as a waiter in Canby's house. Sally lived with him and referred to him as her husband (Yellow Jim had died some years previously). She bore yet another child, a boy named Charles, whose father she identified as a French shopkeeper living nearby. Canby summed up her conduct by saying that Sally, while in her service, behaved so badly that she was a "nuisance to the neighborhood." Miller added that when he sold Sally to Belmonti he did so "in consequence of her profligate habits, by which the peace of my family was disturbed." [17]

Miller issued a plea to his fellow Louisianans to not believe the appalling charge his former slave leveled against him—that of knowingly holding a white woman in bondage. He claimed that he had owned hundreds of slaves over the past thirty years, treating them indulgently and freeing many (including a man he referred to only as Sally's husband—likely Jim Bigger). Miller raised a legitimate point: what would have been his motive in knowingly enslaving a white girl? He had wealth enough to purchase as many slaves as he needed. Furthermore, his mother had cared for white orphans previously, and they had all left her home when they grew up.[18]

Miller made two points in closing. First, he declared his motivation in publishing his side of the story and suing his former slave for fraud: "I am unwilling that the 'finger of scorn' should be pointed at me as a man capable of holding in bondage a white child of tender years entitled to her freedom, for the sake of whatever trifling value her services could ever be to me." He cared deeply for his reputation but even more so for that of his aged mother. Miller now dropped a bombshell. Not only had he completely traced the history of his slave Sally (formerly known as Bridget), he also had discovered, living in the northeastern part of the state, the real Salomé Muller. Miller closed his statement with a challenge: "I am now ready. I court further investigation; I dare my enemies to another trial; I pity, and despise them."[19]

Waiting for the Circuit Court suit to work its way to the top of the docket was not enough for Miller. In a District Court petition dated December 17, Miller launched his own suit against Sally for fraud. He argued that the "person so styling herself Sally Miller well knew that she was not of free birth" and that she had been rightfully held in slavery. He charged that the testimony of her cousins Eve Schuber and Daniel Miller was false and asked that the Court's judgment be revoked, "having been obtained through fraud and ill practices." The fraud, he averred, had only come to his attention after the Court's initial decision and publicity relating to the case. As a result, he had obtained information helping to prove that his former slave had her origins in slavery. More shocking, he had discovered the *real* Salomé Muller, along with her sister Dorothea, living in Morehouse Parish in the northernmost part of the state.[20]

The fraud case would not go to trial until January 1848, but in the meantime, the suit for damages was proceeding in the Circuit Court in a fashion clearly damaging to Sally. In December 1845 and January 1846, depositions were taken from thirteen witnesses who recalled two "Dutch" girls who lived with the families of Thomas Grayson of Boeuf Prairie and later John Thomasson of Monroe. By May, four more depositions had been collected from people who knew the slave Bridget, her owner John Wilson of Alabama, and the circumstances of her sale in New Orleans. Miller and his agents had been busy re-creating the missing years in the life of Salomé Muller the immigrant girl and Bridget/Sally the mulatto slave.[21]

Commissioner Copeland Hunt traveled to the northeastern part of the state to interview people who remembered the arrival of two German orphans in the area in 1818. The witnesses included the four grown children of Thomas Grayson: his son Wiley Grayson and married daughters Betsey Stewart, Narcissa Garrett, and Lucetta Rutland. Grayson himself had since died, but his children had been living in Boeuf Prairie in 1818, and all recalled their father bringing two girls from New Orleans that spring. Many of the details they gave matched the history of Salomé Muller as recounted by the German witnesses from the first trial. The girls' names were Sally and Dorothy, their father was a shoemaker, they were six to eight years old, they spoke Dutch (German), their mother had died on the voyage here, and their father had died suddenly on the journey from New Orleans. (Garrett remembered hearing that he had died of a broken heart after the death of his little boy.) Thomas Grayson paid five hundred dollars for the family's time and brought them to Boeuf Prairie on a keel boat, which he was in the habit of taking to New Orleans for trading. The girls stayed with the Graysons for only a short time before being moved to the home of John Thomasson.[22]

The two apparently suffered at the hands of Mrs. Thomasson during the some seven years they lived and worked as servants there. Many witnesses referred to hearing that the girls were abused, but Monroe lawyer Robert McGuire provided the most graphic detail of the abuse, stating that "When the girls lived at Thomasson's it was commonly reported about town that Mrs Thomasson treated them very cruelly. It was said that she cut the girls with a large kitchen knife and would stick the [illegible] fork in them." As a result, some local people complained to the parish judge, Oliver Morgan, who had the girls brought before him and took testimony from witnesses. McGuire recalled that a verdict had not been rendered; rather, the Thomassons had simply relinquished custody of the girls, who were then taken in by another couple, John and Charlotte Gleason.[23]

The Gleasons confirmed that Sally and Dorothy came to live with them when they were about nine or ten and twelve to fourteen, respectively. Sally had left their home after about a year and a half. Polly, as Dorothy was known, stayed for a year and later married John Parker. They were married for over a decade, until Parker's death. Polly had recently married David Moore. Both the Gleasons stated that they knew Mrs. Polly Moore, now residing in Morehouse Parish, as the former Dorothy Muller.[24]

Needless to say, it was Polly Moore's testimony that was most damaging to the plaintiff's case. All of the other witnesses had known the missing Muller girls, but now here was someone claiming to *be* one of those
missing girls. She related that she did not know her exact age but thought it to
be about thirty-two. She remembered coming to Boeuf Prairie on a boat from
New Orleans with Thomas Grayson and later moving to the Thomassons'.
Her parents, Daniel and Dorothea Muller, were dead, and she was with her
sister, Dorothy, who was two years younger at the time. She remembered
the Graysons calling her Dorothy and her sister Salomé, but said that they
had gotten the names reversed. She, the witness, was actually Salomé.
Mrs. Grayson had also simplified their names to Sally and Polly.[25]

The voyage from Europe was "like a dream," she recalled, with her
mother dying on board ship, seasick and starving. Her father died of unknown
causes as they traveled up the Black River. Moore remembered him eating
a hearty dinner and then lying down and making a strange noise; when she
went to him, he was dead. Her older brother had died in New Orleans, either
by drowning or because "somebody persuaded him off" the ship. Neither
she nor her sister had any birthmarks on their thighs. Her sister had died
three years ago at her house on the Ouachita River.[26]

The final piece of the story of Salomé Muller came from one of her
cousins, Mrs. Dorothy Brown, of Madison Parish. The former Dorothy
Kirchner, she was the daughter of Christopher Kirchner and Salomé Muller,
Daniel Muller's sister, presumably the one for whom his daughter Salomé
was named. Brown stated that her father had been the godfather of one of
the girls and her mother the godmother of the other. Dorothy Kirchner came
over with the others in 1818 when she was fifteen. She recounted the now-
familiar story the New Orleans immigrants had told throughout the earlier
trials. She remained in New Orleans for about a year and then lived for a
year at a plantation three miles below the city. She married and lived in
Claiborne County, Mississippi, for about ten years before moving to
Madison Parish.[27]

She refuted the testimony of Eve Schuber, a schoolmate of hers in
Langensultzbach, saying that on no occasion did Schuber nurse the Muller
girls. In fact, Brown stated, Schuber "paid but little attention" to them.
Rather, their father cared for them after the death of their mother. She had
never heard of any marks on either girl. Since Brown gave her testimony
while visiting New Orleans, Sally's lawyer, Wheelock Upton, had an oppor-
tunity to cross-examine her. He focused particularly on establishing a griev-
ance between her and Eve Schuber. Asked if she liked and respected the

Grubb family (her pronunciation of Kropp, Eve's maiden name), "she said she preferred to keep that to herself." When pressed, she refused to elaborate, but said it had nothing to do with the case before the Court.[28]

Dorothy Brown had last seen Daniel Muller ten days before he and his family left New Orleans and later heard that they had gone by keel boat up the Ouachita River. In 1820, she met butcher Philip Prill, who was driving his cattle from Ouachita to the city market; he reported that the two girls were living on the Ouachita River. Brown and her husband wanted to recover them, but the river was running too high, and there was no steamboat trade going up the river yet. In 1832, she heard that the girls were living in Monroe, and the following year, her brother Daniel Kirchner visited them. He spent about ten days with them in Monroe, recognizing both, saying that one had grown to particularly resemble her mother, a small, delicate woman. Brown corresponded with both cousins, but the one who became Mrs. Hamilton had since died. Brown could not say whether that had been Salomé or Dorothy. She retained locks of hair of the two girls, both of which were auburn and resembled their mother's hair.[29]

Fourteen witnesses so far had helped establish the presence of Salomé Muller in northeastern Louisiana during the time when John Miller's slave Sally was known to be enslaved in the city of New Orleans. Miller's final four witnesses helped to establish the details of her life before this time and the manner in which she came into his possession.[30]

Griffin Holliman, Robert McCarty, and Noel Turner all knew John Wilson and his family in Greene County, Mississippi, on the Alabama border and recalled their owning a slave girl named Bridget. In about 1822, Wilson gave Bridget, described variously as a mulatto or a quadroon, to his married daughter, Mrs. Enoch Rigdon, to act as nurse to her children. Bridget was later sold to a neighbor, Jonathan Thomas. Thomas grew concerned about the legality of his purchase after finding that Wilson had not given his daughter a title to Bridget, so he instructed his son-in-law, Anthony Williams, to take her to New Orleans and sell her.[31]

Much greater detail of Bridget's early life was provided by Mrs. Mary Ann Coward, of Jackson County, Mississippi, who was deposed while visiting New Orleans in January 1846. She was one of the eight children of John and Margaret Wilson. The Wilsons moved from Georgia to Alabama in 1810, where they settled on the Tombigbee River.[32] With them came three slaves: Candice; her one-year-old baby, Bridget; and Candice's mother, Rachael. Rachael was described as a "black guinea negro," Candice as a "mulatto," and Bridget as a "quadroon, her father being a white man."

Coward noted that both Candice and Rachael were still living, although she described Rachael as over one hundred years old, entirely blind, and "of no use to anyone."[33]

When she was about thirteen, Bridget was given to Coward's sister, but was then sold in June 1822 by the sheriff for payment of a debt. Jonathan Thomas, the buyer, sold her about a month or two later to his son-in-law, Anthony Williams. They both lived near Coward, and all attended the same church. Coward described Bridget at the time of the sale as "a common size girl for her age—she was nothing but a girl—had no appearance of the woman about her." The sale of a young child apart from her mother was not common, but the chance of separation increased as a child neared work age. Fifteen to twenty-five was the peak age of slave sales, with girls generally being sold earlier than boys because they could become valuable house servants in their teens.[34]

Coward testified that from the time of Bridget's birth until her sale in New Orleans, a week had not passed without Coward seeing her; thus, she could identify her former slave easily. Bridget, Coward said, was obviously of mixed racial background, with dark auburn hair and dark hazel eyes. She added, "It was not very easy to discover the African blood in her—but it could be discovered in noticing her walking about the house." Coward also offered, without being asked, the information that Bridget had certain marks that would enable Coward to know her. They were like raspberries, one on the inside of each thigh. Bridget also had another mark on her arm, caused by her upsetting a spinning wheel when she was two; the spindle had gone through her arm.[35]

Coward next recounted to Miller's lawyers a very strange incident. The previous night, she related, she had gone with her nephews to the Schubers' house in Lafayette to see the plaintiff in the case. She had tried to see Sally three nights in a row but had been told on each occasion that she was out. Finally, Coward was admitted, Eve Schuber telling her that she could see Sally Muller upstairs. Three women were in the room, and Schuber pointed at the lightest one and identified her as Sally. The room was dark, said Coward, and she had difficulty seeing. She said, "If that is Sally Muller, then it must be so, but if that is you, Bridget, then you should be ashamed of yourself." The three women laughed and then pointed to one of the other women, saying *she* was Sally Muller. This woman had her back to Coward and her hand to her face and would not speak. They all came downstairs, and Coward got a closer look but could not decide if the woman was Bridget. She put her hand on the woman's arm, saying, "If it is you, Bridget,

I can know you by certain marks even if I cannot recognize your face." The woman made no reply.[36]

The record of the lawsuit ends here. It is likely that, seeing the evidence Miller was amassing in his favor, Upton decided to abandon the Circuit Court case. Assuming he had genuinely believed his client's story before, he was now forced to seriously question the trust he had placed in her. But for whatever reason—perhaps he still believed her, had agreed to work on her behalf as long as he was paid, or felt compelled to maintain a public front of support—he continued to serve as her lawyer in the fraud case.

That case went to trial in January 1848. Miller's attorneys offered several crucial documents as evidence of fraud. Most important, they had obtained the indenture agreement of the Muller family from 1818, showing them bound to Thomas Grayson of Boeuf Prairie. The document, dated April 2, 1818, and drawn up by notary John Lynd, showed that Daniel Muller, age thirty-seven; son Jacob, age ten; daughters Dorothea, age eight, and Salema, age four; agreed to "bind and put themselves servants" to Grayson. Daniel Muller owed three years of labor, and his children had to serve until they reached adulthood—in the case of Jacob, to age twenty-one; for the girls, to age eighteen. In return, Grayson agreed to pay the debt they owed to Captain H. H. Bleeker of the ship *Lady Joanna* for their passage to this country. Their new master was also obliged to provide them with "sufficient meat, drink, apparel, washing, and lodging, medicines, medical attendance, education for the minors according to law, and all other necessities fitting such a servant." The contract refers to "articles of agreement entered into, and dated Amsterdam, the second day of December, 1817, between Captain H. H. Bleeker of the ship Lady Joanna . . . in consideration of passage from Amsterdam aforesaid to a port in these United States of American well and strictly to pay or cause to be paid to the said Captain Bleeker of good and lawful money."[37]

The Mullers may not have known what they were agreeing to nor felt they had any choice, for by December, having been trapped in Den Helder for four months, they were desperate. It is also possible that there was no agreement. John Kendall hypothesized in his 1939 account of the case, "Shadow Over the City," that the supercargo or captain may simply have claimed that the passengers were redemptioners and been believed by authorities.[38]

Miller also provided not only the bill of sale showing that he had purchased the slave Bridget from Anthony Williams but also the bill showing her sale from Jonathan Thomas to Williams on July 11, 1822, and the bill from

Enoch Rigdon to Jonathan Thomas, dated July 1, 1822. Miller also provided the deposition of Mrs. Polly Moore, the former Dorothea Muller, taken in New Orleans in May 1846, for the Circuit Court suit.[39]

Testimony in the fraud case against Sally began in court on January 4 and lasted only two days. Defense witness Eve Schuber was the first to be questioned. Much of her account was a summary of her earlier testimony in the first trial. But two new issues were raised. The first had to do with the encounter with Mary Ann Coward, daughter of John Wilson, the original owner of Bridget. In Schuber's account, Coward mistakenly identified Mrs. Clara Letters, Salomé Muller's second cousin (their grandfathers were brothers), as the slave she knew as Bridget. Schuber said that she, her daughter, Letters, and Sally were all in the room at the time. Coward was insistent that Letters was Bridget, even after being contradicted by her two nephews. Clara Letters supported Schuber's statement, saying that she was present when Mrs. Coward came to Schuber's and called her Bridget. When they went downstairs, the two men said she was mistaken because the woman was too young to be Bridget, to which Coward replied that she must be Bridget's daughter.[40]

The second issue had to do with Sally's legal team. The cross-examination of Eve Schuber attempted to throw doubt upon her memory. Schuber could not recall whether the first lawyer who had questioned her about the case four years ago was large or small, whether he wore glasses or not, nor what his hair color was. Naturally, she was asked, if she could not recollect this, how then could she remember a child she last saw twenty-eight years ago? She replied, by her marks and her face.[41]

Miller's lawyers also tried to show that she had had difficulty finding counsel to take on Sally's case. Two attorneys, Isaac T. Preston and L. J. Sigur, testified that they had been consulted by Sally and Eve Schuber regarding the case.[42] Preston said that he had been ready to bring the suit, but other counsel had been employed. Sigur said that he had begun the suit and had met numerous times with the two women in Lafayette but had been replaced by another lawyer before the trial started. Preston and Sigur were called as witnesses for the plaintiff, John Miller, but did not particularly help his case. Preston could not recall whether he had been told about the birthmarks or not, and Sigur would not answer the question on grounds of attorney-client privilege. Eve Schuber stated that she had told Preston about the marks before the suit began. She said that she had never met Sigur nor his partners Bonford and Caperton. She was unclear as to why neither Preston nor Sigur brought the suit forward. Schuber testified that J. C. Wagner, another German immigrant, had been part of the earlier discussions with Isaac Preston. Perhaps Wagner had terminated Preston's service, had contacted Sigur, but had not communicated this to Schuber. Yet Sigur definitely recalled meeting with Schuber on more than one occasion. Whatever the explanation, the confusion did not make Eve Schuber appear to be a reliable witness.[43]

The jury of twelve white men, after discussing the case all night, concluded that they would never come to agreement and were dismissed by Judge Buchanan, who rendered his own decision in their stead. Miller might have been hoping for a repeat of the favor the judge had earlier shown him; but if so, he was disappointed. This time Buchanan returned a verdict against Miller, writing simply that the plaintiff had not successfully made his case for fraud. Within weeks, Miller filed for appeal in the State Supreme Court.[44]

Miller must have been shocked at Buchanan's decision. The judge had earlier decided in his favor but now, after Miller had supplied much more factual material to support his case, the judge turned against him. Miller proceeded to barrage the Supreme Court with evidence. If one witness (Polly Moore) claiming knowledge of the real Salomé Muller was not enough, Miller now presented dozens. In a lengthy (thirty typed pages) brief, Miller's lawyers presented a chain of evidence they believed was now beyond challenge. Where earlier accounts had provided only pieces of the pasts of Salomé the German girl and Sally the slave, Miller now presented an entire life history for each. By agreement, testimony taken from the District Court suit as well as the Circuit Court suit was entered into the record. All this evidence, Miller believed, would finally prove "glaring fraud and deception on the part of the defendant, and of perjury on the part of the principal witnesses, unparalleled in the annals of our jurisprudence."[45]

Eve Schuber was clearly the most important of Sally's witnesses so Miller's attorneys set out to dismantle her testimony, trying especially to cast doubt on her memory. First, they noted, she had failed to recognize her schoolmate, Mrs. Brown, the former Dorothy Kirchner. They had been the same age, been educated and confirmed in the church together, and traveled on the same ship to this country as teenagers. Schuber sat only a few feet away from Brown in Wheelock Upton's office to hear her deposition taken yet did not know her. If Schuber could not recognize Kirchner after twenty-five years, how could she possibly accurately identity a woman she had last seen at age four and who was now a grown woman and the mother of four children of her own?[46]

Schuber also could not recall which lawyers she had consulted in the case—or, as the prosecution implied, she *could* recall and lied about it. Her testimony contradicted that of lawyer L. J. Sigur, who stated that he had met Schuber and Sally several times at their house in Lafayette and, he thought, at his office, too. He stated clearly that he believed himself to be acting as their attorney and that he expected to be paid by Schuber. Schuber, on the other hand, claimed never to have met Sigur or his partners. In court, on the grounds of professional privilege, Sigur had refused to answer the question of whether he had been told about the birthmarks on the person of Salomé Muller. Miller argued there could only be one reason for Sigur's unwilling-ness to respond and that was because he knew Schuber was lying when she claimed to recall such marks on Salomé. Or, as Miller wrote, "Mrs. Schuber only remembered that the child, Salomé Muller, had peculiar marks when she found such proof was necessary, in the opinion of her legal advisers, to maintain her pretensions." [47]

The defendant's response was brief, covering three points. First, wrote Sally's attorney Wheelock Upton, no suit to annul a judgment of the Supreme Court could be maintained in the District Court. In other words, the original fraud suit had been illegitimate in the first place. Second, Upton disputed Miller's claim, arguing that there had been no fraud, the prosecu-tion witnesses were honest, and the Supreme Court, in the previous appeal, had believed them. Third, the burden of proof was on the plaintiff to show that the defendant was descended from a slave mother, and he had failed to do so. [48]

The Supreme Court hearing this case was an entirely different court from the one that had first declared Sally free in 1845. The 1845 state con-stitutional convention had reorganized the Court, and on March 19, 1846, a new court assembled. The members now were Pierre Rost, George Eustis, George Rogers King, and Thomas Slidell. Eustis and Rost had briefly served on the Court in 1839, but Martin's opposition to them (they had been appointed to help expedite the caseload) forced their resignations. A member of the 1845 convention, Eustis now became chief justice of the new Court. Originally from Boston, he had served previously as Louisiana secretary of state. Rost was born in France and had emigrated to the United States, set-tling first in Natchez, where he studied for the bar under Joseph E. Davis (Jefferson Davis's brother). Rost moved to New Orleans and set up a law practice, also becoming a sugar planter. [49] George Rogers King was from Opelousas and had served in the Louisiana House of Representatives, as a district attorney, and also as district judge of the Court of Criminal Errors and Appeals. The brother of U.S. senator and later Confederate agent John Slidell, Thomas Slidell came from New York to establish a law practice in New Orleans. He later served in the state senate. In 1852 he was elected to a ten-year term as chief justice, defeating Christian Roselius. But when Slidell was assaulted at the polls during the 1855 elections, he sustained injuries that forced him to retire.[50]

This Court delivered its opinion of the case in May 1849. In it, Judge Pierre Rost gave two reasons for the dismissal of Miller's case. First, the Court agreed with Upton that no suit to annul a judgment of the Supreme Court (referring to the previous decision in which Sally was declared free) could be maintained by a lower court.[51] Even if the Court had supported Miller's claim, Sally's restoration to bondage would have been extremely unlikely. The Louisiana Supreme Court tended to follow the dictum that once a slave had been declared free, that freedom could not be revoked.[52] Second, Miller's role in the suit was questioned. Belmonti, "the real party in interest," had not joined the appeal and apparently had accepted the earlier judgment. Since Miller had not refunded Belmonti the money he had paid for Sally, he "had no interest in contesting the former decree and therefore, no capacity to do so." In other words, Louis Belmonti, who had lost the seven hundred dollars he had paid for the slave, might have had a reason for challenging the decision, but John Miller did not.[53]

In fact, Miller did have an interest in seeing the case overturned, although it was not financial. In his petition, he claimed that the trial had resulted in the "throwing upon himself and upon his aged mother, in the minds of many, who do not know them, the suspicion of having been parties to an act which, had they really committed it, would have justly made them objects of scorn and reproach to the community." [54] From its inception in 1844, the case had attracted much publicity, especially in New Orleans, a city with a large number of newspapers. William Turner, John Miller's former business partner, had stated during the first trial that the case "had been the town talk for some months." [55]

This publicity had even prompted Miller, during the course of the first trial, to defend himself in the press. Southern white men placed great value on their honor, and when this honor was questioned, a response was mandatory. To fail to publicly rebut an accusation of impropriety was to admit defeat. As Edward Ayers has written, southern men knew "that the failure to respond marked them as less than real men, branded them, in the most telling epithets of the time, as 'cowards' and 'liars.' " [56] In a statement printed in the *Picayune*, Miller related the circumstances of Salomé Muller's life as he had heard them reported as well as those of his slave Bridget, a different person altogether. He emphasized that, until his former slave brought her lawsuit, he had "never heard of any claim of freedom being made by her." Nor did he believe her to be anything other than a mulatto slave. Miller reminded the public that he had been a respectable resident of New Orleans for thirty-six years and stated that anyone who knew him could not possibly believe him guilty of the crime of which he was charged.[57]

That crime was a very serious one indeed. Miller and his mother stood accused of one of the worst offenses in American society, that of knowingly holding a white person in bondage. Miller had been bested publicly by a woman, a former slave, his obvious social inferior. He had been humiliated. It was this final point that the Supreme Court addressed. The best the judges could do for his reputation was to note that "To the observation of counsel that the only object of the plaintiff in bringing the suit was to vindicate his character . . . we have carefully perused the new evidence discovered by him; that it stands in the record unimpeached, and is in direct conflict with that adduced by the defendant in the former suit to prove her birth and condition. If it can be true that the defendant is of German extraction, we consider the plaintiff as exonerated of all knowledge of that fact."[58]

In a petition for rehearing, Miller's lawyers argued that, when he joined Belmonti in the first case as warrantor, he had become, in effect, the real defendant. Miller, then, had a right to appeal the decision.[59] There is no record of this suit going forward. Quite possibly, Miller simply ran out of funds or was persuaded by his lawyers or friends that there was no longer any point in pursuing the case.

Conclusion

$\mathcal{T}$he evidence indicates that Sally Miller and Salomé Muller were in fact two different people. Certainly, the story of a German immigrant's enslavement in the United States seems farfetched. But it wasn't impossible. People of wholly European descent did sometimes find themselves enslaved. One could argue that it was more implausible that a slave of African descent had managed to convince so many people that she was actually white. For white New Orleanians such deception was unimaginable. Most whites in both the North and the South believed that racial traits were immutable. In a person of mixed racial background, even the faintest trace of African blood would make itself known in some manner. Whites needed to believe this because racial identity was tied to status and privilege. To maintain the racial hierarchy the white elite had created, people could not be able to pass unnoticed from one group to another. The idea of a white person's enslavement was shocking and frightening but perhaps less so than the thought that a lifelong slave of African descent had deceived southerners and slipped seamlessly into white society.

Courtroom testimony in the first trial revealed substantial evidence to support the slave Sally's claim that she was in fact Salomé Muller. Six witnesses who knew Salomé as a little girl either testified that Sally resembled the Muller family or identified her specifically as the missing girl. Some of these witnesses were relatives of the Mullers or close friends who had traveled with them to the United States. They remembered specific details about her appearance such as the birthmarks on her thighs.[1] Their testimony was emotional and heartrending, but it was also persuasive. Even today, despite scientific studies revealing that eyewitness testimony is frequently unreliable, many remain convinced that an eyewitness provides the most accurate description of an event.

Not everyone, however, was impressed with the prosecution witnesses. Judge Alexander M. Buchanan wrote that the defense witnesses were numerous and respectable; on the other hand, he completely dismissed the testimony of two of the prosecution witnesses.[2] An unattributed handwritten note on the printed copy of Sally's lawyer Wheelock Upton's motion for a new trial said, "The distinction between the witnesses of the plaintiff and defendant is this—plaintiff's witnesses are second table witnesses—defense witnesses live in the parlor—parlor witnesses are most credible." The idea that testimony from working-class people had been unfairly discounted was addressed in Upton's appeal to the Supreme Court: "Of all that poor & half starved people who came over to this country in the Bark Johanna, in 1818, & who now survive, I tell the Court there is not one, except this unfortunate Plaintiff, who is not in better than middling circumstances—all of them are well off, many of them really affluent."[3] John Miller had even harsher words for the German witnesses than Buchanan did. Some observers had suggested that Sally's supporters were dupes taken in by her tale of woe, but he preferred to see them as malicious, writing, "Their evidence bears marks of a well concocted and unprincipled scheme devised by one or more persons, to defraud me, put money in their pockets and gratify the bad feeling of a very bad servant, and obtain for themselves a temporary notoriety." He dismissed Upton, too, as a fame-seeking abolitionist.[4]

Against the Germans' identification of Sally as Salomé, however, was Miller's documentation that Sally was in fact a legally purchased slave. No one disputed that she had been a slave for her entire adult life, and slave status clearly implied African ancestry. But since she had only come into his possession at the age of twelve, her early history was unknown and thus could have coincided with Salomé Muller's. The prosecution had not proven how the young German child had been enslaved, but it did not have to. The Supreme Court judges agreed that John Miller had not illegally enslaved her. But someone else might have.

In the first Supreme Court appeal, the judges focused their attention exclusively on "the great question which the pleadings present, to wit, whether the plaintiff be white and free, or a slave."[5] If Sally were shown to be white, she would go free; if black, she would remain in slavery. How, then, was her race to be determined? Antebellum judges and juries had several factors to consider when deciding an individual's race. They could look at personal history: what was known of a person's ancestry—particularly, whether she or he had been born to a slave mother. Scientific evidence of black blood might not be immediately apparent to the untrained eye, but doctors familiar with the allegedly different physiognomies of the races knew what specific traits to look for. Physical appearance was relevant as well: did the person *look* white? And related to appearance was performance: did a person *act* white, and was he or she accepted as white by other whites?[6]

Not until the Circuit Court trial did Sally's ancestry come into the debate. In depositions, her former owners from Alabama defined her as a quadroon, having one-quarter African ancestry. Her mother, Candice, was described as a mulatto; her grandmother, Rachael, as a "black guinea negro," perhaps an indication that she was born in Africa.[7] During the original trial and appeal, however, no one involved knew the circumstances of Sally's background. Appearance was the sole focus of the attempt to determine her race.

Not surprisingly, the prosecution witnesses at the trial thought Sally looked white. Most believed she resembled the German girl they remembered from so long ago, but there were also a few who had only known her in this country, such as Miller's neighbor Madame Poigneau. Poigneau testified that Sally's appearance marked her as white.[8] Upton's description of his client—"long, straight black hair, hazle [*sic*] eyes, Roman nose, and thin lips"—certainly was consistent with that of a white person. Upton further explained that, if Sally's complexion appeared somewhat dark, it was a result of longtime exposure to the sun. The parts of her body that remained clothed were "of that peculiar whiteness which is never found in the African descendant."[9] More compelling, though, were the *defense* witnesses who frankly admitted she looked like a white person.

Mrs. Ann Kopman, who lived with Sarah Canby during the late 1820s, gave her opinion that, when young, Sally had looked white, although not German.[10] A frequent visitor to Miller's, Jonathan L. Lewis, described Sally's physical appearance as being "as white as most persons" but declared that he had seen other slaves as "bright" as she. Yet appearance was not an absolute; it was always interpreted through the lens of a person's beliefs about the nature of race. Although he had once thought that Sally had a somewhat "colored" appearance, upon reflection Lewis concluded that, because he had seen her only in the company of other slaves, he had *assumed* her to be a slave and therefore black. Miller's notary Carlile Pollock judged that Sally was of mixed blood from her complexion. But when asked if he had seen her in the company of white girls, would he have believed her to be white, Pollock could not deny that he would indeed have believed so. He added, "There are in New Orleans many white persons of dark complexion & many colored persons of bright complexion." Yet Pollock clung to the common notion that somehow, inexplicably, people could tell the difference between black and white. The court reporter noted of Pollock that "being asked what there is in the features of a colored person that designates them to be such, says he cannot exactly say. That persons who live in countries where there are many colored persons acquire an instinctive means of judging that cannot be well explained." [11]

Performance was another aspect of appearance and served as an additional means of judging Sally's race. As Judge William Harper wrote in an 1835 South Carolina case, the proportion of black or white blood obvious from physical appearance was not the only correct way to identify a person. One needed also to consider the individual's reputation, his or her reception in society, and whether he or she exercised the rights of white people. [12] To Upton, the fact that Sally *appeared* white to others meant that she *was* white. In his appeal to the Supreme Court, he noted that

> the perseverance, the uniform good conduct, the quiet and constant industry, which are found in those she claims as relatives, have always been found in her, and however polluted and degraded her person may have been, these traits have yet left her worthy of the relatives who ask her at your hands—*and these traits prove her white nature*, and so too does the fact that she has made herself the friends whom she has made, and that these friends seem to be bound to her as it were by very "hooks of steel." I argue, then, that both morally and physically, she shows before the Court that there is nothing of the African about her. [emphasis in original] [13]

The high level of support Sally had garnered in the white community, then, proved that she must be white:

> *It is, sir, to shew her moral power, and weight, and influence. An influence, which I contend no one but a white woman could possibly raise up and control—an influence as inconsistent with the nature of an African, as it would be with the nature of a Yahoo.* I contend that the moral traits of the Quartronne, the moral features of the African taint are far more difficult to be erased, and are far more easily traced, than are the distinctions and differences of physical conformation. The Quartronne is idle, reckless and extravagant, this woman is industrious, careful, and prudent—the Quartronne is fond of dress, of finery and display—this woman is neat in her person, simple in her array, and with no ornament upon her, not even a ring on her fingers. [emphasis in original] [14]

Additionally, for women, a successful white performance lay in depicting themselves as pure, embodying female honor.[15] This was perhaps why Sarah Canby focused on Sally's sexual misbehavior, as evidenced by her bearing four children by four different men, including two who were black. In her contribution to the pamphlet her son had published to defend himself, Canby denounced Sally as "an abandoned character" even at the early age of fourteen.[16] Jonathan L. Lewis also explained how Sally's sexual behavior affirmed her blackness, testifying in court that "if she had been white it would not have been permitted that she should live as the wife of this colored boy."[17]

Ariela Gross, in her study of cases of nineteenth-century racial identity, argues that Sally successfully depicted herself as white.[18] She displayed character traits associated with whites and convinced respectable white people to accept her as one of their own. After her discovery by Madame Karl in 1843, Sally lived with the Schubers in Lafayette and drew members of the German-American community to her side. Gross adds that the success of women such as Sally represented the achievement of a universal ideal of womanhood that included beauty as well as purity.[19] But while other women in similar cases were consistently described as attractive, Sally was not. And while it is likely that Sally was in a sexual relationship with Louis Belmonti and was perhaps even purchased for that reason, there is no reference to her anywhere as a "fancy girl." Most descriptions refer to her as plain and stocky rather than beautiful. Only one newspaper stated that Sally "when young must have been pretty good-looking."[20]

According to Gross, freedom suits based on racial identity were fairly common throughout the antebellum South. Scholars have looked extensively at the laws governing race, which made the concept seem more defined than it was in reality. Less attention has been given to trials. Legislatures tried to reduce race to a binary system, but court cases show it was more complex. Southern whites might have believed in racial essence, but they could not agree how to determine it. Law was important in defining race, but throughout the antebellum era, performance of whiteness became more important. Appearance was crucial because juries made the racial determinations in most nineteenth-century cases and were more likely to believe what their eyes told them rather than a complicated formula based upon an individual's ancestry.[21]

Gross argues that it was "easiest to prove one's whiteness in Louisiana." Such cases occurred here more frequently than anywhere else in the country because of the state's tolerance for gradations of color.[22] According to

John Blassingame, "By the time Reconstruction began, miscegenation had been going on for so long that more people of both the 'white' and 'Negro' populations in New Orleans and Louisiana had ancestors in the other race than did the residents of any other city or state in America. In fact, the population was so mixed that it was virtually impossible in many cases to assign individuals to either group."[23] Frederick Law Olmsted, visiting New Orleans in the early 1850s, related a bewildering array of degrees of racial complexity as used by the city's French population:

sacatra—griffe and negress

griffe—negro and mulatto

marabon—mulatto and griffe

mulatto—white and negro

quarteron—white and mulatto

metif—white and quarteron

meamelouc—white and metif

quarteron—white and meamelouc

sang-mele—white and quarteron

Olmsted added that experts claimed to be able to distinguish among these varieties.[24] Perhaps visitor Benjamin Latrobe put it best when he was asked to describe the New Orleans population. He replied that one might as well ask, "What is the shape of a cloud?"[25]

Both Sally and her legal opponent revealed the extent to which race was a social construct that placed a person's identity in the hands of others. In her original petition to the Court, Sally claimed that Miller had "in violation of all law human and divine, converted [her] into his slave . . . reducing her in all things to the level and condition of that degraded class."[26] Conversely, Miller argued that "She has metamorphosed by the 'Grace of God' and the decision of the Supreme Court . . . from Sally Miller, my former Slave, into Salome Muller, a free white German redemptioner."[27]

What did their contemporaries think? The New Orleans press reported on Sally's case, generally taking the line that her situation, if true, was horrible but clearly unusual or, as the *Picayune* put it, "unparalleled." When the first trial ended in Miller's favor, the same paper expressed relief that his good reputation had not been damaged.[28] The abolitionist press did not exploit the Miller case as much as might have been expected. Sally's story could readily have served as a vehicle for frightening whites into a more personal understanding of the threat that slavery presented to all Americans, not just blacks. But perhaps abolitionists assumed that the general public would simply disregard the case as a curiosity, its extraordinary nature merely reaffirming the belief that slavery posed no threat to the average white person.

An editorial in the *Pennsylvania Freeman* reveals the attitude of some abolitionists toward cases of alleged white slavery. Referring to the *Picayune*'s calling of Sally's situation "an unparalleled case of cruelty and oppression," the *Freeman* answered that the case was "a most horrible and fiendish act of cruelty, but by no means an 'unparalleled' one. It has its *millions* of parallels in this country, differing from no particular except the color of the skin." Several months later, the *Freeman* again discussed the case, this time responding to a *Philadelphia Ledger* piece promoting compensation for Sally for her illegal enslavement. The *Freeman* argued, "But what claim does the color of the skin give to any one for compensation for services?" [29]

Antislavery advocates may have agreed, perceiving that a focus on one instance of white enslavement was irrelevant while millions of blacks remained in bondage. Or worse yet, concern for Sally might even play into slaveholders' hands: opposition to illegal enslavement could imply support for legal enslavement. White abolitionists may have found the fear of white enslavement remote, exaggerated, or, because of the implied commonality between blacks and whites, offensive. While most northern whites would have found the case disturbing for any number of reasons, it probably caused few to become fearful for their own safety. The reality of southern slavery was personally as well as geographically remote.

Another issue may have played a part in abolitionists' reluctance to use Sally's case as propaganda. Mary Niall Mitchell, in her analysis of photographs of "white slaves" sold as *cartes de visites*, has shown that the most popular images were those of female children. Children, especially girls, were society's most vulnerable members, those most in need of protection and thus most likely to inspire white northern conversion to the abolitionist cause. Children were innocent, as yet untouched by slavery's evils. What such propaganda asked viewers to do was to save them from leading lives of bondage.[30] Sally Miller, thirty-four years old when the trial began, had spent her life in slavery and was marred by it. Through no fault of her own, she had been debased by slavery, and this debasement, to antebellum

FIGURE 9. "Emancipated slaves, white and colored." 1864. *Picture Collection, The Branch Libraries, The New York Public Library, Astor, Lennox, and Tilden Foundations.*

whites, significantly included bearing four children out of wedlock, at least two of them by nonwhite men.

Sally's case may not have had much value for the abolitionist cause, but it did have dramatic value; and writers of both fictional and nonfictional accounts of the case began publishing within a few years of the final judgment. Most writers (including this one, initially) supported Sally's version of events, accepting her white status based on the Supreme Court's 1845 decision, apparently unaware of the evidence that later cases produced.

William Wells Brown was the first non-journalist to write about the case, incorporating it into his novel *Clotel*. Brown was a fugitive slave from Kentucky who established himself in Buffalo, New York, where he became a conductor on the Underground Railroad. In 1847, he published his autobiography and embarked on a career as an international spokesman for the abolitionist movement.[31] In 1853, he turned his hand to fiction. *Clotel* tells the story of Currer, the mulatto mistress of Thomas Jefferson, and their daughters Clotel and Althesa. Sally Miller's story was portrayed through the character of Salomé, a slave hired by Althesa, who has been purchased by a white man she later marries. When Althesa questions the slave's sadness, she hears an amazing story. Salomé was born in Germany, came to New Orleans with her parents, and began working as a nurse. Her father died of yellow fever, and she lost her job when her employers left town. She was kidnapped by two men, who took her up the Yazoo River, where she was enslaved on a farm and made to bear three children by another slave. She was then transferred to her owner's daughter, who brought her to New Orleans. When Althesa and her husband try to help the unfortunate woman, her owners remove her, but she is discovered three months later by a fellow German who helps initiate a lawsuit for her freedom. Eventually, Salomé wins her freedom, although her three children remain in bondage. "This, reader," Brown affirmed, "is no fiction." [32] Brown either got some of the details wrong or simply did not know them and filled in his own version. But he clearly based the story on Sally Miller. According to William Farrison, Brown's purpose in including her account was not to arouse sympathy for enslaved whites but to highlight the potential dangers to everyone of a system that had no respect for human rights.[33]

Another slave-turned-abolitionist, William Craft, mentioned Sally's case in his account of his and his wife's 1848 escape from slavery in Georgia. Craft began his narrative by establishing his wife Ellen's white appearance (her father was her master) and noted that white-looking, and in fact wholly white slaves, were not out of the ordinary. Because slaves could not testify against whites in most courts, however, they had no recourse to prove their identity. Craft related, "I have myself conversed with several slaves who told me that their parents were white and free; but that they were stolen away from them and sold when quite young." He offered Sally's case as an example. His largely accurate account, taken from the prosecution testimony at the first two trials, included a description of the Germans' voyage to this country, Sally's enslavement by John Miller, her rediscovery in New Orleans, and Belmonti's claim that Miller knew she was white.[34]

George Washington Cable provided the first full version of the case. His article, "Salome Müller, The White Slave," was published in *Century Magazine* and in Cable's collection *Strange True Stories of Louisiana*, both in 1889. Cable was a controversial figure in postwar New Orleans. Born in 1844, he served in the Confederate cavalry and after the war worked at various jobs, including clerking at the Cotton Exchange and writing for the *Picayune*. At some point, Cable's views on race began changing from those of a typical white southerner to a civil rights advocate. His first public stance against segregation—when a group of nonwhite students was expelled from Girls' High School—came in 1875.[35] Cable's account of the Sally Miller case was one of his first forays into nonfiction writing. His outline was basically correct, although he got some details wrong (calling Madame Karl Sally's cousin, listing Sally as having three children, naming her daughter as the child who died) and embellished others (creating conversations, such as Sally's response to Madame Karl, "I am a yellow girl").[36] He used the trial transcripts as well as interviews with some of Sally's friends and relatives, although he specified neither whom nor what they told him.[37] Cable is best known for popularizing New Orleans and its people as a literary subject, and developing the image familiar to many, with emphasis on the city's exotic flavor.[38] His treatment of Sally's case is consistent with this representation; it obviously qualified as a "strange true story." But it was also written at the time of Cable's racial crusade; he was perhaps trying to show southerners that the system of racial categorization—which had lived after slavery had ended—was invalid.

Contemporary to Cable's version was J. Hanno Deiler's recounting of the case. Deiler was a professor of German at Tulane University who published an article on Sally in Germany in 1888 and revised it in 1901. Reverend Louis Voss translated Deiler's work and published his own summary of the case, based on Deiler's and Cable's accounts, in the *Louisiana Historical Quarterly* in 1929.[39] Deiler was a proponent of German immigration who sought to restore the shipping connection to New Orleans that had been discontinued in 1882, thus ending the continual infusion of German culture into the Crescent City. (He had almost succeeded on the eve of World War I.)[40] Deiler and Voss were both concerned with preserving the history of the city's German population. Deiler based his version of the case on the pamphlet written by Sally's lawyer, Wheelock Upton (which Cable does not mention). Unlike Cable, Deiler apparently did not have access to the court records. By drawing upon both Deiler and Cable, Voss gave a fairly accurate summary of the case through the first Supreme Court decision and one that was essentially sympathetic to Sally.[41]

Ten years after Voss's article, Sally Miller was again the subject of an article in the *Louisiana Historical Quarterly*. In "Shadow Over the City," John Kendall included the case of Sally Miller as an illustration of the life of a slave. He argued inaccurately that neither slaves nor free blacks had the ability to tell their stories, so he employed Sally, reflecting, "how interesting it would be to have a record of the feelings and ideas of a white man or woman living and thinking as a slave; in reality neither slave nor black, yet believing himself or herself to be both!" Kendall added, however, that Sally may or may not have been white, and in any event, she did not tell her own version of events. Kendall's summary of the case was largely correct but did not include events that occurred after 1845. He was the first author, though, to raise the possibility that Sally was not who she said she was. He argued that while her case left room for doubt, the Supreme Court justices feared the retention of a white woman in slavery more than the accidental freeing of a mulatto slave.[42]

John Bailey's more recent account of the case, *The Lost German Slave Girl*, is based on more extensive research than previous treatments have been. Bailey's account of the case is semi-novelized and speculates on some of the interactions that occurred between Sally and the other participants in the trial. He concludes that Sally was in fact not the missing German immigrant.[43]

Sally Miller's case was not the last of its kind that the Louisiana State Supreme Court would confront. In 1861, the Court heard the case of Alexina Morrison, who like Sally alleged that she was a white woman held illegally in slavery. Morrison claimed that she had been born of white parents in Arkansas and was then kidnapped and enslaved in New Orleans. The first trial ended in a mistrial when the jury declared itself unable to reach a verdict, but she was successful the second time her case came before the District Court. Morrison's owner, James White, appealed the decision, arguing that he had purchased her legally and that she had not been able to prove her whiteness, relying only on witnesses' claims that she looked white. Interestingly, Christian Roselius, one of Sally's legal team, here represented the slaveholder.[44]

On the surface, the legal issue was simple. If white, Morrison was free; if black, she was a slave; if neither was proven, she was a mulatto and assumed to be free. The reality, however, was more complicated. Determining the race of a person of obviously mixed background was difficult enough, but Morrison's owner faced the challenge of convincing jury members not to believe their own eyes. Morrison was blond, blue-eyed, and light-skinned. The slaveholder's argument that black blood could be present in an individual without being visible forced southern whites to confront their greatest fear—that amalgamation would over time allow all people with black ancestry to blend in with the white population. As Walter S. Johnson has written, "a virtuoso performance of whiteness could breach the categories designed to contain and commodify hybridity; a slave could step over the color line and onto the other side." Not only did this imply that partially black slaves could perform whiteness so well that it became reality, but it also challenged the biological assumption of race. If one could *perform* whiteness, race clearly was not scientifically determined.[45]

The Supreme Court voided the jury verdict and returned the case to the District Court after finding that some of the defense evidence had been improperly excluded. The opinion was written by Judge Alexander M. Buchanan, who had presided over the first *Miller v. Belmonti* case in District Court and had since been appointed to the Supreme Court. Buchanan indicated what he expected the verdict to be, writing that Morrison was "proved to be of fair complexion, blue eyes, and flaxen hair. But the presumption of freedom, arising from her color, is not a presumption *juris et de jure*. It must yield to proof of a servile origin." In a third trial, however, a jury again found in Morrison's favor. Her owner appealed, but the case stalled after the federal occupation of New Orleans. What happened to Morrison is unknown. By 1862, when the second appeal was lodged, she was in jail and apparently in poor health.[46]

Like Alexina Morrison's, Sally's case revealed the difficulty of trying to define an indefinable quality. The varying verdicts in both cases show that, despite what southern whites might have wanted to believe, knowing who was black and who was white was anything but easy. What is perhaps most surprising is the fact that southern courts did not uniformly side with powerful owners against powerless slaves. Although their support for the slave system and racial hierarchy in general was manifested in their rigorous legal code, when dealing with individuals, southern whites could put aside their own society's rules.

Ariela Gross's study of cases of racial determination reveals that, of the twelve lawsuits involving women that she studied, eleven were won by the plaintiffs; the other ended in a hung jury. She argues that women's success came from their ability to embody the values expressed in the Victorian Cult of True Womanhood. Such cases were more frequent in Louisiana, and claimants stood a greater chance of proving whiteness here than elsewhere in the antebellum South.[47]

That fact may seem surprising given that Louisiana was and still is imagined to embody the most inhumane aspects of the institution of slavery. No other place in the South provided as much fodder for abolitionists and was attacked accordingly. These attacks were based on the image of large gangs of slaves toiling endlessly in cotton and sugar fields. Evidence came from newspaper accounts of desperate runaways, shockingly high death rates, and advertisements offering dogs bred to hunt slaves. New Orleans was particularly targeted for its role as a major trading center, exposing practices such as selling children away from their parents and selling women for sexual partners.[48]

It seems obvious that Louisiana was determined to keep its black population enslaved. The legislature was busy during the antebellum era, passing laws to restrict emancipation in various ways, including an 1852 act mandating that any slaves freed had to be sent out of the country to Liberia at the owner's expense. Five years later, manumission was simply prohibited. But as Judith Kelleher Schafer has shown, this did not prevent emancipation from occurring. The legislature, weary of hearing petitions to exempt people from 1852 act, revised it in 1855, handing over the decision to the District Courts. The volume of cases (159 suits involving 289 slaves in slightly more than sixteen months) indicates that many New Orleans slaveholders wanted to free their slaves and allow them to remain in the state. Every slave freed in the New Orleans District Courts in 1855 and 1856 successfully petitioned to remain in Louisiana. At a time when southern whites increasingly viewed manumission as an act of sedition, New Orleans juries were systematically letting slaves go free.[49]

A decade earlier the Courts had faced the question of whether to liberate one particular slave. Why did the Supreme Court allow Sally Miller to go free? The first trial and appeal produced much evidence in her favor. But the later trials seriously damaged her case, a result of the information John Miller had uncovered about his slave's early life as well as Salomé Muller's. Why, then, did she remain free? The Court was undoubtedly reluctant to re-enslave someone who had been freed. As a free woman, Sally posed no danger to the populace of New Orleans. John Miller suffered no financial loss when she was declared free, and the Court did what it could for his reputation, stating clearly that he had not been the one to enslave her initially. Louis Belmonti, who had lost his 750-dollar purchase price, was from a lower class and a different ethnic background from the judges; thus, they perhaps felt no empathy for his loss. And there was some question as to Sally's role in Belmonti's household. Perhaps the Court viewed Belmonti as not really losing a slave worker but simply a sexual partner, a role that she could have continued once free, if she so chose.

Finding in favor of John Miller, and re-enslaving Sally on the strength of the evidence produced in the later trials, would have been an admission of error by the Court. It was surely easier to think of her as the tragic victim of fate rather than a successful racial con artist. The notion of white enslavement was shocking, but the vision of Sally as a kidnapped German child was less frightening overall than the alternative—an African slave who had tricked whites; who had triumphed over the system; who had bent white law, public opinion, and the Courts to her will. A slave passing for white, writes Gross, represented "the most disturbing deceit."[50] Gender is at the heart of the matter as much as race. It was possible to comprehend a woman, a little girl really, at the mercy of powerful white men—an awful situation but a familiar one. But a black woman taking on such power by demanding and claiming her freedom when legally she was not entitled to it: that was an image antebellum whites would not have found acceptable.

After the legal battle with his former slave ended in 1849, John F. Miller returned to his comfortable estate and position as one of the leaders of New Iberia society. There he remained active in local affairs, such as the effort to restore the St. Martin Parish courthouse. In September 1853, the parish "solons" adopted a resolution sponsored by Miller advocating the establishment of a three-member committee to estimate the cost of repairs to the 1840 building.[51] But he did not remain out of the legal system for long. In 1850, he was sued by a neighbor, François Duplessis. Both Miller and Duplessis had claimed woodland lying between their lands. The Supreme Court argued that both sides had weak claims, neither having taken possession of the land, occupied it, or enclosed it. Nor did either have a title to the land at the time of the American takeover of the Louisiana Territory. But based on Spanish land claims, Miller held the earlier confirmation, so the case was decided in his favor.[52]

Miller died in New Iberia on December 3, 1857, and was buried in Rosehill Cemetery.[53] But even after his death, his involvement in the Courts continued. One case was brought in 1860 by Harvey Beach, one of Miller's creditors from the time of his insolvency. In the St. Martin District Court, Beach argued that he had been one of those creditors scheduled for payment when Miller became bankrupt but had never been paid. The lower court's decision—that once a person had been discharged from bankruptcy, further claims could not be made on him or his heirs—was affirmed by the Supreme Court.[54]

Litigation involving Miller did not end here. In his will, he had left his considerable estate to his niece Cordelia Wheeler Lewis, daughter of his sister Mary Ann. But Wheeler's good fortune came with strings attached. She apparently acquired some debt along with her uncle's wealth and so began selling off parts of the estate, including Butte à Peigneur, in 1859.[55] And the New Iberia plantation was soon the subject of litigation, part of the land claimed by Myra Clark Gaines. Well known in Louisiana, Gaines had been in one court or another since 1834, trying to win recognition as Daniel Clark's only legitimate child, which would have made her heir to a huge fortune in New Orleans and the surrounding region. In 1866, Gaines sued Lewis to recover the part of Miller's plantation that had once belonged to Clark. Eventually, a compromise was reached and resulted in the sale of the land to Lewis in 1869. Gaines died in 1885, but her case remained in litigation until 1891, when the final judgment awarded her estate slightly more than half a million dollars.[56]

What happened to Sally and her children is less clear. Eve Schuber testified in the second District Court trial that Sally had lived with the Schubers in Lafayette for about a year after being discovered. She then moved out and lived alone in the Third Municipality.[57] According to George Washington Cable, at some point she married and divorced John Given, a Mississippi River pilot. Her sons, whom Cable incorrectly claimed became free when she did, went to Tennessee and Kentucky, where they were "heard of once or twice as stable boys to famous horses."[58] Louis Voss gave a different account, writing that she went to Sacramento, California, with her white husband Frederick King, where her cousin Henry Schuber saw her in 1855.[59]

Throughout the story, a voice is missing: that of the main character in this drama, Sally herself. Although their voices might have been heard through the work of others, virtually every other person connected to the case communicated in some way: through a newspaper article, court testimony, or a deposition. Only Sally remains completely silent. Was it because she had no memory of her early life and enslavement and thus her testimony was unnecessary from a legal point of view? Was it because she was a slave—and a female one at that—in a society that relegated blacks and women to the background, letting white men speak and make decisions for them? Or was it because she knew she was perpetuating a fraud and shrewdly figured that the less she said, the better? Deborah Gray White has written that slave women understood the value of silence and secrecy; they had to hide their true feelings to survive.[60] For Sally Miller, this may have been doubly true. Silence was part of the coping strategy she had learned as a slave, and it became the price of her freedom.

NOTES

INTRODUCTION *The Discovery of Salomé Muller*

1. Trial transcript, *Sally Miller v. Louis Belmonti and John F. Miller* (called in warranty), no. 23,041, First District Court of Louisiana, 24 January–25 June 1844, Supreme Court of Louisiana Collection, Earl K. Long Library, University of New Orleans (hereafter referred to as *Miller v. Belmonti* 1844).

2. Trial transcript, *Sally Miller v. Louis Belmonti and John F. Miller* (called in warranty), no. 5,623, Supreme Court of Louisiana, 13 July 1844–30 June 1845, Supreme Court of Louisiana Collection, Earl K. Long Library, University of New Orleans (hereafter referred to as *Miller v. Belmonti* 1845).

3. Ibid.

4. The Attakapas prairie region in the south-central part of Louisiana was a center for cattle raising as well as plantation farming. Today it is encompassed by the parishes of St. Mary, Iberia, Vermillion, St. Martin, and Lafayette.

5. The Faubourg St. Mary was the neighborhood just above the Vieux Carré (the original settlement, or French Quarter), beginning at Canal Street. Also known as the American District, it was inhabited mainly by American rather than French Creole residents. Lafayette, which included the modern Garden District, was a separately incorporated city just above the Faubourg St. Mary. See Joan B. Garvey and Mary Lou Widmer, *Beautiful Crescent: A History of New Orleans*, 4th ed. (New Orleans: Garmer, 1982), 90–91; and Meloncy C. Soniat, "The Faubourgs Forming the Upper Section of the City of New Orleans," *Louisiana Historical Quarterly* 20 (1937): 192–211.

6. *Miller v. Belmonti* 1844.

7. To avoid confusion between Sally Miller and her previous owner, John Miller, I have decided to use the familiar first name to refer to Sally. It is how she, as a slave, would have been referred to in her time. The last name attributed to her was John Miller's. By contrast, I refer to Salomé Muller exclusively as Salomé, although she was called Sally, to avoid confusion between the two.

8. *Miller v. Belmonti* 1844. The redemption system was a type of indentured servitude that developed among German-speaking immigrants in the early

eighteenth century. Immigrants who were unable to pay overseas passage signed contracts with merchants in Europe who agreed to pay their passage. The immigrants then had a specified amount of time to get family or friends at the port of debarkation to reimburse their costs; they were then freed, or "redeemed." If the money was not paid within the allotted time, the new arrivals were auctioned off as indentured servants. See chapter 4 for a further discussion of redemptioners.

9. Liliane Crété, *Daily Life in Louisiana, 1815–30*, trans. Patrick Gregory (Baton Rouge: Louisiana State University Press, 1981), 43, 56–57.

10. *Miller v. Belmonti* 1844. Slave sales balanced the rights of buyers and sellers, unlike other commodities in the antebellum economy, where caveat emptor prevailed. All southern states had laws regulating slave sales, but Louisiana provided buyers with more protection under what were called redhibition laws. *Redhibitia*, a Roman legal concept, referred to the canceling of a sale because the product had defects hidden at the time of sale. Such laws regulated the terms of warranty—what sellers guaranteed a buyer—and included physical or mental defects, disease, and character flaws, such as a tendency to run away, a common "character defect" found in slaves. Then as now, a warranty was a seller's way of communicating to buyers that the seller would take responsibility for a product's quality. Warranties could be implied rather than explicitly stated, and courts tended to interpret the concept of warranty broadly in slave sales. Simply advertising a slave as healthy or sound often implied a warranty. But sales of human beings were more nuanced than were sales of goods and livestock; the qualities of human chattel were not always readily apparent to potential buyers. And a slave had the power to affect sales by behaving in a certain manner; his or her actions could facilitate a sale to one buyer and then deter purchase by another. Such complexity resulted in frequent warranty litigation over slave sales. See Jenny Bourne Wahl, *The Bondsman's Burden: An Economic Analysis of the Common Law of Southern Slavery* (New York: Cambridge University Press, 1998), 27–35; Walter S. Johnson, *Soul by Soul: Life Inside the Antebellum Slave Market* (Cambridge, Mass: Harvard University Press, 1999), 12, 131, 176–87; Ariela J. Gross, *Double Character: Slavery and Mastery in the Antebellum Southern Courtroom* (Princeton, N.J. Princeton University Press, 2000), 6, 54; and Kenneth M. Stampp, *The Peculiar Institution: Slavery in the Ante-Bellum South* (New York: Vintage, 1956), 241–43, 252–53.

11. *Miller v. Belmonti* 1844.

12. Ibid.

13. Ibid.

CHAPTER 1   *A Slave Sues Her Master*

1. Leonard V. Huber, *New Orleans As It Was in 1814–15* (New Orleans: Battle of New Orleans 150th Anniversary Committee of Louisiana, 1965), 4–10; Judith Kelleher Schafer, "Slaves and Crime: New Orleans, 1846–62," in *Local Matters: Race, Crime and Justice in the Nineteenth Century South*, ed.

Christopher Waldrep and Donald G. Neiman (Athens: University of Georgia Press, 2001), 68–69; A. Oakley Hall, *The Manhattaner in New Orleans* (1847; reprint, Baton Rouge: Louisiana University Press, 1976), 78.

2. Glenn R. Conrad, ed., *A Dictionary of Louisiana Biography* (New Orleans: Louisiana Historical Association, 1988), 2:696–97; Louis Voss, *Louisiana's German Heritage: Louis Voss' Introductory History*, ed. Don R. Tolzmann (1927; reprint, Bowie, Md.: Heritage Books, 1994), 63–64. For a more personal impression of Roselius, Grymes, and other prominent lawyers and judges, see [John Smith Whitaker], "Sketches of the Life and Character in Louisiana—The Portraits Selected Principally from the Bench and Bar" (New Orleans: Ferguson and Crosby, 1847).

3. Robert Tallant, *The Romantic New Orleanians* (New York: Dutton, 1950), 95–97; Conrad, *Dictionary of Louisiana Biography*, 1:363; Elizabeth Gaspard, "The Rise of the Louisiana Bar: The Early Period, 1813–1839," *Louisiana History* 28 (1987):196; Joseph G. Tregle, Jr., *Louisiana in the Age of Jackson* (Baton Rouge: Louisiana State University Press, 1999), 127–28. Because antebellum New Orleans's legal community was small and concentrated, the opposing counsel would have been familiar with one another. Most attorneys kept offices within a six-block square bounded by Royal, Old Levée, Canal, and Bienville streets, convenient to the courthouse. See Gaspard, "Rise of the Louisiana Bar," 188, 192.

4. *Miller v. Belmonti* 1844.

5. *Digest of 1808*, title 6, chap. 3, p. 30; *Civil Code of 1825*, article 177, p. 28, in Judith Kelleher Schafer, *Slavery, the Civil Law and the Supreme Court of Louisiana* (Baton Rouge: Louisiana State University Press, 1994), 220–21; Judith Kelleher Schafer, " 'Guaranteed Against the Vices and Maladies Prescribed by Law': Consumer Protection and the Law of Slave Sales, and the Louisiana Supreme Court, 1809–1862," *American Journal of Legal History* 31 (October 1987): 306. In addition to appearing in court to claim their freedom, slaves could also be tried when accused of crimes. They could testify for or against fellow slaves but not against whites.

6. Gross, *Double Character*, 41.

7. *Miller v. Belmonti* 1844.

8. Ibid.

9. Ibid.

10. Ibid.

11. Conrad, *Dictionary of Louisiana Biography*, 1:563; John Duffy, ed. *The Rudolph Matas History of Medicine in Louisiana* (Baton Rouge: Louisiana State University Press, 1958), 2:11–12, 46.

12. *Miller v. Belmonti* 1844.

13. Ibid; *Michel and Co. New Orleans Annual [Directory] and Commercial Register for 1846* (New Orleans: E. A. Michel and Company, n.d.).

14. John S. Kendall, *History of New Orleans* (Chicago, 1922) 2:363; Tregle, *Louisiana in the Age of Jackson*, 33; Sarah Searight, *New Orleans* (New York: Stein and Day, 1973), 99.

CHAPTER 2   *The Mullers of Alsace*

1. Copies of the birth certificates are found in trial transcript, *John F. Miller v. Sally Miller*, no. 1,114, Supreme Court of Louisiana, 14 June 1848–21 May 1849, Supreme Court of Louisiana Collection, Earl K. Long Library, University of New Orleans (hereafter referred to as *Miller v. Miller* 1849).

2. *Miller v. Belmonti* 1844.

3. Marianne S. Wokeck, *Trade in Strangers: The Beginnings of Mass Migration to North America* (State College: Pennsylvania State University Press, 1999), xxi, n. 2; Liliane M. Vassberg, *Alsatian Acts of Identity* (Philadelphia: Multilingual Matters, 1993), 9.

4. *Miller v. Belmonti* 1844.

5. John F. Nau, *The German People of New Orleans, 1850–1900* (Leiden: E. J. Brill, 1958), 2–3; Mack Walker, *Germany and the Emigration, 1816–1885* (Cambridge, Mass: Harvard University Press, 1964), 1, 6–7, 30–31.

6. Wokeck, *Trade in Strangers*, 1–6; Stanley Nadel, *Little Germany: Ethnicity, Religion and Class in New York City, 1845–1880* (Urbana: University of Illinois Press, 1990), 15–16; Bruce Levine, *The Spirit of 1848: German Immigrants, Labor Conflict and the Coming of the Civil War* (Urbana: University of Illinois Press, 1992), 22; Carl A. Brasseaux, "French Immigration, 1820–1839," in *The Louisiana Purchase Bicentennial Series in Louisiana History*, ed. Carl A. Brasseaux, vol. 10: A *Refuge for All Ages: Immigration in Louisiana History* (Lafayette: University of Southwestern Louisiana Press, 1996), 336.

7. LaVern J. Rippley, *The German-Americans* (Boston: Twayne, 1976), 40; Walker, *Germany and the Emigration*, 3; Aaron S. Fogleman, *Hopeful Journeys: German Immigration, Settlement, Political Culture in Colonial America, 1717–1775* (Philadelphia: University of Pennsylvania Press, 1996), 21, 23; Brasseaux, "French Immigration," 336.

8. Rippley, *German-Americans*, 40; Farley W. Grubb, "The End of European Immigrant Servitude in the United States: An Economic Analysis of Market Collapse, 1772–1835," *Journal of Economic History* 54 (December 1994): 798, 813; Nadel, *Little Germany*, 16; C. Edward Skeen, "The Year Without a Summer: A Historical View," *Journal of the Early Republic* 1 (spring 1981): 58. In Switzerland, 1816 was known as the "year of the beggars' mortality." See André Jardin and André-Jean Tudesq, *Restoration and Reaction, 1815–1848*, trans. Elborg Forster (New York: Cambridge University Press, 1983), 39.

9. Walker, *Germany and the Emigration*, 4–6; Skeen, "Year Without a Summer," 58; Jardin and Tudesq, *Restoration*, 39.

10. Walker, *Germany and the Emigration*, 2, 4–5, 33; Jardin and Tudesq, *Restoration*, 23, 39; Geoffrey Ellis, *The Napoleonic Empire* (New York: Macmillan, 1991), 60.

11. Rippley, *German-Americans*, 40; Walker, *Germany and the Emigration*, 2; Walter D. Kamphoefner et al., eds., *News from the Land of Freedom: German Immigrants Write Home*, trans. Susan Carter Vogel (Ithaca, N.Y.: Cornell University Press, 1988), 2; Levine, *Spirit of 1848*, 24; Nadel, *Little Germany*, 16; Ellis, *Napoleonic Empire*, 106.

12. Brasseaux, "French Immigration," 336; Michael Broers, *Europe Under Napoleon, 1799–1815* (London: Arnold, 1996), 191.

13. Wokeck, *Trade in Strangers*, 5; Brasseaux, "French Immigration," 336; Dan P. Silverman, *Reluctant Union: Alsace-Lorraine and Imperial Germany, 1871–1918* (State College: Pennsylvania State University Press, 1972), 10–11; Jardin and Tudesq, *Restoration*, 22.

14. Brasseaux, "French Immigration," 336.

15. Wokeck, *Trade in Strangers*, 3–4.

16. Walker, *Germany and the Emigration*, 7; Thomas W. Page, "The Transportation of Immigrants and Reception Arrangements in the Nineteenth Century," *Journal of Political Economy* 19 (1911): 732–33; Fogleman, *Hopeful Journeys*, 34–35; Anita M. Mallinckrodt, *From Knights to Pioneers: One German Family in Westphalia and Missouri* (Carbondale: University of Southern Illinois Press, 1994), 115.

17. Walker, *Germany and the Emigration*, 29–30; Agnes Bretting, "Organizing German Immigration: The Role of State Authorities in Germany and the United States," in *America and the Germans: An Assessment of a 300-Year History*, ed. Frank Trommler and Joseph McVeigh (Philadelphia: University of Pennsylvania Press, 1985), 1:27–28.

18. *Miller v. Belmonti* 1844.

19. Ibid.

20. Walker, *Germany and the Emigration*, 27–28, 20–21; Voss, *Louisiana's German Heritage*, 77; Bretting, "Organizing German Immigration," 25.

21. *Miller v. Belmonti* 1844.

22. Ibid. There is some confusion over the captain's name and position. Various sources refer to the ship's captain as Gransten, Grandsteiner, or Krahnstover. I have relied on the name most frequently used by witnesses in the court records, Grandsteever. Whether he actually captained the ship is unclear. Court witnesses testified that the Mullers traveled on a ship captained by Grandsteever, but the Mullers' indenture agreements name their captain as Bleecker. New Orleans newspapers referred to Grandsteever as the ship's supercargo, an officer on a merchant ship in charge of commercial concerns.

23. Page, "Transportation of Immigrants," 740.

24. Paul Wilhelm, Duke of Württemberg, *Travels in North America, 1822–24*, ed. R. Nitske and S. Lottinville (Norman: University of Oklahoma Press, 1973), chap. 1.

25. Voss, *Louisiana's German Heritage*, 76. Even for well-off passengers, the trip could be tedious. Emil Mallinckrodt, who in 1831 journeyed from Germany to New Orleans, wrote to his cousin Gustav that the trip was exceedingly boring. "If one sees nothing but water for five weeks and is shut up in a box for eight, then when one is released one hops about with happiness like a bird." See Mallinckrodt, *From Knights to Pioneers*, 118.

26. Page, "Transportation of Immigrants," 737.

27. "Passenger List of the Ship 'Elizabeth' Which Arrived at Philadelphia in 1819," *Pennsylvania Magazine of History and Biography* 25 (1901): 255–56.

28. Page, "Transportation of Immigrants," 738, 741; Friedrich Kapp, *Immigration and the Commissioners of Emigration of the State of New York* (1870; reprint, New York: Arno, 1969), 23, 24.

29. Page, "Transportation of Immigrants," 738–39; Kapp, *Immigration*, 19–26; Farley W. Grubb, "Morbidity and Mortality on the North Atlantic Passage: Eighteenth Century German Immigration," *Journal of Interdisciplinary History* 17 (1987): 565, 569, 572.

30. Grubb, "Morbidity," 573; Kapp, *Immigration*, 25–26; Page, "Transportation of Immigrants," 739.

31. *Miller v. Belmonti* 1844.

32. "Passenger List of the Ship 'Elizabeth,'" 255–56; Kapp, *Immigration*, 25.

33. "Report of Andreas Geyer, Jr., on the Condition of German Redemptioners on Board of the American Ship *General Wayne*, Captain John Conklin, Addressed, on April 27, 1805," *Records of the German Society of Philadelphia*, in Kapp, *Immigration*, 183–86; also reprinted in Edith Abbott, ed. *Immigration: Select Documents and Case Records* (Chicago: University of Chicago Press, 1924), 11–13.

34. *Niles' Register*, 1 November 1817.

35. *Niles' Register*, 31 January 1818; Kapp, *Immigration*, 22.

36. *American Watchman*, 7 January 1818.

37. *Miller v. Belmonti* 1844.

38. Ibid.

39. Ibid; J. Hanno Deiler, "The System of Redemption in the State of Louisiana," trans. Louis Voss, *Louisiana Historical Quarterly* 12 (1929): 439–40.

40. *Louisiana Gazette*, 9 March 1818.

41. *Miller v. Belmonti* 1844.

CHAPTER 3   *New Orleans*

1. Farley W. Grubb, "German Immigration to Pennsylvania, 1709–1820," *Journal of Interdisciplinary History* 20 (winter 1990): 417, 422.

2. Page, "Transportation of Immigrants," 736.

3. Virginia R. Dominguez, *White by Definition: Social Classification in Creole Louisiana* (New Brunswick, N.J.: Rutgers University Press, 1986), 112; Paul Wilhelm, *Travels in North America*, 32–34; Mallinckrodt, *From Knights to Pioneers*, 119; Joseph Logsdon, "Immigration through the Port of New Orleans," in *Forgotten Doors: The Other Ports of Entry to the United States*, ed. Mark Stolarik (Philadelphia: Balch Institute Press, 1988), 107–13.

4. *Balize* (or *balise*) is the French word for "buoy."

5. Frederick M. Spletstoser, "Back Door to the Land of Plenty: New Orleans as an Immigrant Port" (Ph.D. diss., Louisiana State University, 1978), 1:190–95; Amos Stoddard, *Sketches: Historical and Descriptive, of Louisiana* (Philadelphia: Mathew Carey, 1812), 160; Tregle, *Louisiana in the Age of Jackson*, 1.

6. Benjamin Henry Latrobe, *The Journals of Benjamin Henry Latrobe, 1799–1820, From Philadelphia to New Orleans*, ed. Edward C. Carter III,

John C. Van Horne, and Lee W. Formwalt (New Haven, Conn.: Yale University Press, 1980), 3:viii–ix.

7. Paul Wilhelm, *Travels in North America*, xiii–iv.

8. Mallinckrodt, *From Knights to Pioneers*, 117, 121.

9. Paul Wilhelm, *Travels in North America*, 22–23.

10. Latrobe, *Journals*, 3:160; Paul Wilhelm, *Travels in North America*, 23–25.

11. Mallinckrodt, *From Knights to Pioneers*, 119.

12. Harold Sinclair, *The Port of New Orleans* (Garden City, N.Y.: Doubleday and Doran, 1942), 161, 197–98; Charles Dufour, *Ten Flags in the Wind: The Story of Louisiana* (New York: Harper and Row, 1967), 153. Timothy Flint put the number of steamboats at fifty in 1822. See Timothy Flint, *Recollections of the Last Ten Years in the Valley of the Mississippi*, ed. George R. Brooks (1826; reprint, Carbondale: Southern Illinois University Press, 1968), 222.

13. Mallinckrodt, *From Knights to Pioneers*, 119.

14. Spletstoser, "Back Door to the Land of Plenty," 1:202; Mallinckrodt, *From Knights to Pioneers*, 119; Paul Wilhelm, *Travels in North America*, 24, 30; Latrobe, *Journals*, 3:163–64; Tregle, *Louisiana in the Age of Jackson*, 2–3.

15. Paul Wilhelm, *Travels in North America*, 31.

16. Ibid., 14.

17. *Miller v. Belmonti* 1844.

18. David Goldfield, *Cotton Fields and Skyscrapers: Southern City and Region, 1607–1980* (Baton Rouge: Louisiana State University Press, 1982), 30.

19. Bennett H. Wall et al., *Louisiana: A History*, 3d ed. (Wheeling, Ill.: Harlan Davidson, 1997), 106–12; Garvey and Widmer, *Beautiful Crescent*, 69.

20. J. G. Flügel, "Pages from a Journal of a Voyage down the Mississippi to New Orleans in 1817," ed. Felix Flugel, *Louisiana Historical Quarterly* 7 (1924): 427; Mallinckrodt, *From Knights to Pioneers*, 119.

21. Sinclair, *Port of New Orleans*, 166; Anonymous, *Biographical and Historical Memoirs of Louisiana* (Chicago: Goodspeed, 1892) 1:179, 181; Spletsoser, "Back Door to Plenty," 1:206.

22. Anonymous, *Biographical and Historical Memoirs*, 1:180; Dennis Rousey, *Policing the Southern City: New Orleans, 1805–1889* (Baton Rouge: Louisiana State University Press, 1996), 12; Huber, *New Orleans As It Was*, 3; Kendall, *History of New Orleans*, 2:674, 743.

23. Kendall, *History of New Orleans*, 2:672; Bernard Lemann, *The Vieux Carré: A General Statement* (New Orleans: Samuel Wilson, Jr., Publications Fund of the Louisiana Landmarks, 1966), 11; Sinclair, *Port of New Orleans*, 168.

24. Anonymous, *Biographical and Historical Memoirs*, 1:179, 181; Jessie Poesch and Barbara Bacot, eds., *Louisiana Buildings, 1720–1940* (Baton Rouge: Louisiana State University Press, 1997), 41–43; Stoddard, *Sketches*, 152–53; Huber, *New Orleans As It Was*, 3, 43–44; William Darby, *A Geographical Description of the State of Louisiana* (Philadelphia: John Melish, 1816), 185–87.

25. Rousey, *Policing the Southern City*, 12; Stoddard, *Sketches*, 153; Darby, *Geographical Description*, 185–87; Estwick Evans, "A Pedestrious Tour, of Four Thousand Miles Through the Western States and Territories During the

Winter and Spring of 1818," in *Early Western Travels, 1748–1846*, ed. Reuben G. Thwaites (1819; reprint, Cleveland: Arthur H. Clark, 1904), 337–38; Huber, *New Orleans As It Was*, 30; Leonard V. Huber, *New Orleans: A Pictorial History* (Gretna, La.: Pelican, 1991), 107.

26. Wall et al., *Louisiana*, 36–37; Evans, "Pedestrious Tour," 337–38; Huber, *New Orleans As It Was*, 16; Rousey, *Policing the Southern City*, 12; Robert Baird, *View of the Valley of the Mississippi*, 2d ed. (Philadelphia: H. S. Tanner, 1834), 278; Flint, *Recollections*, 214, 321; Henry Brackenridge, *Views of Louisiana* (Pittsburgh: Cramer, Spear, and Eichbaum, 1814), 176; John C. Guillet and Robert N. Smith, *Louisiana's Architectural and Archeological Legacies* (Nachitoches, La.: Northwestern State University Press, 1982), 122. The old meat market now houses the Café du Monde.

27. Dominguez, *White by Definition*, 104, 106; Wall et al., *Louisiana*, 73–74.

28. Evans, "Pedestrious Tour," 339–40; Sinclair, *Port of New Orleans*, 167–68; John G. Clark, *New Orleans, 1718–1812: An Economic History* (Baton Rouge: Louisiana State University Press, 1970), 313.

29. Duffy, *Medicine in Louisiana*, 1:352, 358–60, 372–76; Gaillard Hunt, *As We Were: Life in America, 1814* (1914; reprint, Stockbridge, Mass.: Berkshire House, 1993), 207–9; Flint, *Recollections*, 214.

30. Stoddard, *Sketches*, 170; Paul Wilhelm, *Travels in North America*, 34; Duffy, *Medicine in Louisiana*, 1:354, 407–8; Charles Sealsfield [Karl Pöstl], *The Americans as They Are: Described in a Tour Through the Valley of the Mississippi* (London: Hurst, Chance, and Company, 1828), 175, 193. Karl Pöstl, born in Moravia, traveled the United States and then returned to Europe to become a best-selling novelist under the name Charles Sealsfield. Most of his works were about the American Southwest and Mexico. See Ulrich Carrington, *The Making of an American: An Adaptation of Memorable Tales by Charles Sealsfield* (Dallas: Southern Methodist University Press, 1972), ix–x.

31. Gary A. Donaldson, "Bringing Water to the Crescent City: Benjamin Latrobe and the New Orleans Waterworks System," *Louisiana History* 28 (1987): 389–90, 395; Duffy, *Medicine in Louisiana*, 1:406–7; Latrobe, *Journals*, 3:xi.

32. New Orleans's board of health was established the same year as Philadelphia's but later than those of Baltimore, Boston, Charleston, and New York. See Stanley K. Schultz, *Constructing Urban Culture: American Cities and City Planning, 1800–1920* (Philadelphia: Temple University Press, 1989), 120; Duffy, *Medicine in Louisiana*, 1:352–53, 396, 298, 411–13.

33. Duffy, *Medicine in Louisiana*, 1:399–400; Flint, *Recollections*, 225.

34. Duffy, *Medicine in Louisiana*, 1:352–53, 397–99, 411–13; Schultz, *Constructing Urban Culture*, 120.

35. Duffy, *Medicine in Louisiana*, 1:400–2, 405; Logsdon, "Immigration," 109; Anonymous, *Biographical and Historical Memoirs*, 1:121.

36. Evans, "Pedestrious Tour," 336–37; Darby, *Geographical Description*, 187.

37. Wall et al., *Louisiana*, 101, 103–4; Sealsfield, *Americans as They Are*, 184.

38. Sealsfield, *Americans as They Are*, 147–48. *Estaminet* is a French term for "tavern." See Widmer and Garvey, *Beautiful Crescent*, 82; Tregle, *Louisiana in the Age of Jackson*, 20–21; John S. Kendall, "Shadow Over the City," *Louisiana*

Historical Quarterly 22 (1939):150; Evans, "Pedestrious Tour," 336; Wall et al., *Louisiana*, 154.

39. Tregle, *Louisiana in the Age of Jackson*, 21–22; François-Xavier Martin, *The History of Louisiana From the Earliest Period* (1882; reprint, New Orleans: Pelican, 1963), 313; Thomas N. Ingersoll, *Mammon and Manon in Early New Orleans: The First Slave Society in the Deep South, 1718–1819* (Knoxville: University of Tennessee Press, 1999), 251; Alcée Fortier, *The American Domination, 1803–1861*, vol. 3 of *History of Louisiana* (New York, 1904), 198. The college, founded in 1811, never prospered, and closed in the mid-1820s. See Tregle, *Louisiana in the Age of Jackson*, 44–45.

40. Loren Schweninger, "A Negro Sojourner in Antebellum New Orleans," *Louisiana History* 20 (1979): 306–8.

41. Flügel, "Pages from a Journal," 432, 427; Evans, "Pedestrious Tour," 340.

42. Ingersoll, *Mammon*, 251; Crété, *Daily Life*, 44, 54–55.

43. Charles Dufour, "The People of New Orleans," in *The Past As Prelude: New Orleans, 1798–1968*, ed. Hodding Carter (New Orleans: Tulane University, 1968), 37–38; Dominguez, *White by Definition*, 112.

44. The five American cities larger than New Orleans were New York City, Philadelphia, Baltimore, Boston, and Charleston. See Hunt, *As We Were*, 22.

45. Latrobe, *Journals*, 3:166; Darby, *Geographical Description*, 186; Baird, *View of the Valley*, 279, 281; Anonymous, *Biographical and Historical Memoirs*, 1:179; Evans, "Pedestrious Tour," 335–36.

CHAPTER 4 *Germans and Redemptioners*

1. Kendall, *History of New Orleans*, 2:363.

2. Ibid; Tregle, *Louisiana in the Age of Jackson*, 33. There was also a large German settlement in the Faubourg Marigny (see chapter 6).

3. Kendall, *History of New Orleans*, 2:747–49; Frederick S. Starr, *Southern Comfort: The Garden District of New Orleans, 1800–1900* (Cambridge, Mass.: MIT Press, 1989), 5; Soniat, "Faubourgs," 198, 200; Dominguez, *White by Definition*, 119; Tregle, *Louisiana in the Age of Jackson*, 33–34; Martha Ann Brent Samuel and Ray Samuel, *The Great Days of the Garden District and the Old City of Lafayette* (New Orleans: Parents' League of the Louise S. McGehee School, 1961), 9–13; Sealsfield, *Americans as They Are*, 175.

4. Spletstoser, "Back Door to Plenty," 1:9; Robert C. Reinders, *The End of an Era: New Orleans in the 1850s* (New Orleans: Pelican, 1964), 18.

5. Rippley, *German Americans*, 44.

6. Herbert Weaver, "Foreigners in Antebellum Towns of the Lower South," *Journal of Southern History* 13 (1947): 63.

7. Reinders, *End of an Era*, 18

8. Voss, *Louisiana's German Heritage*, 77–78.

9. Logsdon, "Immigration," 107–13. The end of the direct shipping connection between New Orleans and Germany came in 1882. The result was that, without the continual infusion of new immigrants, German culture declined. The German Society, headed by J. Hanno Deiler, a professor of German language at

Tulane University, a propagandist, and an immigrant himself, lobbied aggressively for reestablishment of the shipping link and had almost succeeded when World War I began. See Raimond Berchtold, "The Decline of German Ethnicity in New Orleans, 1880–1930" (M.A. thesis, University of New Orleans, 1984), 11–12.

10. Widmer and Garvey, *Beautiful Crescent*, 22–23; Wall et al., *Louisiana*, 35–39.

11. Widmer and Garvey, *Beautiful Crescent*, 25–26; Wall et al., *Louisiana*, 35–39.

12. *L'ami des lois*, 7 March 1818; *Louisiana Gazette*, 7, 9 March 1818.

13. Voss, *Louisiana's German Heritage*, 77; Page, "Transportation of Immigrants," 744–45.

14. Page, "Transportation of Immigrants," 741–43.

15. Voss, *Louisiana's German Heritage*, 74.

16. *Louisiana Gazette*, 5–11 March 1818. The ship *Juffrow Johanna* was also reported to have arrived at Baltimore with hundreds of passengers in poor condition. This led to the rechartering of the German Society of Maryland in 1818. See Günter S. Moltmann, "The Migration of German Redemptioners to North America, 1720–1820" in *Colonialism and Migration: Indentured Labor Before and After Slavery*, ed. P. C. Emmer (Dordrecht: Martinus Nihoff, 1986), 116–17.

17. Deiler, "System of Redemption," 433. Deiler's account of the case was published in Germany, first in 1888 and then revised in 1901. It was based mainly on the German translation of the 1845 pamphlet written by Sally's attorney, Wheelock Upton.

18. Aaron S. Fogleman, "From Slaves, Convicts, and Servants to Free Passengers: The Transformation of Immigration in the Era of the American Revolution," *Journal of American History* 85 (June 1998): 43.

19. Ibid., 49–51; Moltmann, "Migration of German Redemptioners," 107; Marianne Wokeck, "Harnessing the Lure of the Best 'Poor Man's Country': The Dynamics of German-Speaking Migration to British North America, 1683–1783," in *"To Make America": European Immigration in the Early Modern Period*, ed. Ida Altman and James Horn (Berkeley: University of California Press, 1991), 217–18; Albert B. Faust, *The German Element in the United States* (1927; reprint, New York: Arno Press and the *New York Times*, 1969), 66.

20. Fogleman, "From Slaves, Convicts, and Servants," 60, 62–63; Moltmann, "Migration of German Redemptioners," 106.

21. Kapp, *Immigration*, 9–12; Moltmann, "Migration of German Redemptioners," 108.

22. Kapp, *Immigration*, 9–12; Moltmann, "Migration of German Redemptioners," 108–9; Grubb, "End of European Immigrant Servitude," 797.

23. Deiler, "System of Redemption," 441.

24. Livingston is also known for his decades-long battle to win control over part of the New Orleans batture, the alluvial land between the levée and the river. See Conrad, *Dictionary of Louisiana Biography*, 1:515; and George Dargo, *Jefferson's Louisiana: Politics and the Clash of Legal Traditions* (Cambridge, Mass.: Harvard University Press, 1975), 74–101.

25. Livingston and Grymes also worked together defending the Lafitte brothers on smuggling charges. See William B. Hatcher, *Edward Livingston* (Baton Rouge: Louisiana State University Press, 1940), 214; and Tregle, *Louisiana in the Age of Jackson*, 120. *Miller v. Belmonti* 1844.

26. *Louisiana Gazette*, 14 March 1818.

27. *Niles' Register*, 11 April 1818. Yet only a month later, the same paper blasted a Viennese newspaper for exaggerating the potential problems of American emigration. The *Register* reprinted from this paper a translation of a piece purportedly from Boston that clearly attempted to discourage emigrants from leaving Europe. In it, "several respectable gentlemen" in Boston urged those in Vienna to publicize the horrendous plight of emigrants to the United States. They mention specifically Swiss travelers and Germans from Württemberg and Palatine who had come to Boston in "the most wretched condition." The crowded ships were described as being filled with people in a "half starving condition." While certainly realistic enough, the article's conclusion stretched the truth: "What is called emigrants' land lies at a distance of 3000 English miles from any of the Atlantic states, and the journey thither must be made on foot." The piece added that the United States had no need of artisans because all manufactured goods were imported cheaply, food was very expensive, and during the winter (which lasted seven to eight months) there were no jobs for the poor. See *Niles' Register*, 2 May 1818.

28. Faust, *German Element*, 68–69, 72.

29. "Exploitation of Emigrants by Passenger Brokers," extract from "A Report of a Committee of the American Chamber of Commerce in Liverpool, 1822," reprinted in appendix to *Report from Select Committee on Emigration from the United Kingdom* (1826), in Abbott, *Immigration*, 15–16.

30. Grubb, "End of European Immigrant Servitude," 814; Grubb, "Morbidity," 567; Farley W. Grubb, "The Disappearance of Organized Markets for European Immigrant Servants in the United States: Five Popular Explanations Reexamined," *Social Science History* 18 (spring 1994): 8.

31. Spletsoser, "Back Door to Plenty," 1:25; Brasseaux, "French Immigration," 336–37.

32. Kapp, *Immigration*, 9–12; Deiler, "System of Redemption," 434–35.

33. Reprinted in Deiler, "System of Redemption," 436–37.

34. Sealsfield, *Americans as They Are*, 175.

35. Villeré, who served from 1816 to 1820, was Louisiana's first native-born governor. See Sidney Louis Villeré, *Jacques Philip Villeré: First Native-Born Governor of Louisiana, 1816–1820* (New Orleans: Historic New Orleans Collection, 1981), ix, 88, 91–92; Flügel, "Pages from a Journal," editor's note, 492.

36. Henry A. Bullard and Thomas Curry, *A New Digest of the Statutes of the State of Louisiana* (New Orleans, 1842) 1:693–95; Brasseaux, "French Immigration," 336–37.

37. Grubb, "End of Immigrant Servitude," 794, 799–801, 815, 817; Grubb, "Disappearance of Organized Markets," 1–4, 21–24; Moltmann, "Migration of German Redemptioners," 114.

CHAPTER 5   **Sally and John Miller**

1. *Miller v. Belmonti* 1844.
2. Richard C. Wade, *Slavery in the Cities: The South, 1820–60* (New York: Oxford University Press, 1964), 22; Robert C. Reinders, "Slavery in New Orleans in the Decade before the Civil War," *Louisiana History* 44 (October 1962): 213; Virginia Meacham Gould, " 'If I Can't Have My Rights, I Can Have My Pleasures, and If They Won't Give Me Wages, I Can Take Them,' " in *Discovering the Women in Slavery*, ed. Patricia Morton (Athens: University of Georgia Press, 1996), 184, 185; Laurence J. Kotlikoff and Anton J. Rupert, "Manumission of Slaves in New Orleans, 1827–1846," *Southern Studies* 19 (summer 1980): 177. Whites were not the only slaveowners. In 1830, one in every seven New Orleans slaves was owned by a free black person.
3. John F. Miller, "A Refutation of the Slander and Falsehood Contained in a Pamphlet, Entitled, Sally Miller" (New Orleans, 1845) in *Free Blacks, Slaves, and Slaveowners in Civil and Criminal Courts: The Pamphlet Literature*, ed. Paul Finkelman (New York: Garland, 1988), 15, 55–56; *Miller v. Belmonti* 1844; *U.S. Census*, Louisiana, 1830, 1840; Glenn R. Conrad, "Wilderness Paradise: A Glimpse of Jefferson Island and Its Owners for the Past Two Centuries," *Attakapas Gazette* 15 (1979): 56, note.
4. Wade, *Slavery in the Cities*, 23–24, 30, 121; Goldfield, *Cotton Fields and Skyscrapers*, 46; Gould, " 'If I Can't Have My Rights,' " 180–81; Reinders, "Slavery in New Orleans," 215, Gross, *Double Character*, 32.
5. John A. Eisterhold, "Lumber and Trade in the Lower Mississippi Valley and New Orleans, 1800–1860," *Louisiana History* 13 (winter 1972): 71, 76, 80–82, 87–90; Robert S. Starobin, *Industrial Slavery in the Old South* (New York: Oxford University Press, 1970), 25–26, 40.
6. Conrad, *Dictionary of Louisiana Biography*, 1:570; [Paxton's] *The New-Orleans Directory and Register* (New Orleans: Benjamin Levy and Company, 1822); [Paxton's] *The New-Orleans Directory and Register* (New Orleans: Benjamin Levy and Company, 1823); [Paxton's] *A Supplement to the New-Orleans Directory of the Last Year* (1824); [Paxton's] *The New-Orleans Directory and Register* (New Orleans: A.T. Penniman and Company, 1830); *Michel's New Orleans Annual and Commercial Register . . . for 1834* (New Orleans: Gaux and Sollée, 1833); Roulhac Toledano, *The National Trust Guide to New Orleans* (New York: Wiley, 1996), 98, 104; Mary Louise Christovich et al., *The American Sector*, vol. 2 of *New Orleans Architecture* (Gretna, La.: Pelican, 1972), 79.
7. Miller's mother had been widowed twice, first by his father, John Fitz Miller, Sr., and then by Joseph Canby, both of whom died before she and her son moved to New Orleans.
8. *Miller v. Belmonti* 1844; Richard H. Steckel, "Women, Work, and Health under Plantation Slavery in the United States," in *More Than Chattel: Black Women and Slavery in the Americas*, ed. David Barry Gaspar and Darlene Clark Hine (Bloomington: Indiana University Press, 1996), 44; Wade, *Slavery in the Cities*, 28–31; Wilma King, *Stolen Childhood: Slave Youth in Nineteenth Century America* (Bloomington: Indiana University Press, 1995), 24; Marie Jenkins

Schwartz, *Born in Bondage: Growing Up Enslaved in the Antebellum South* (Cambridge, Mass.: Harvard University Press, 2000), 108; Reinders, "Slavery in New Orleans," 215; Wade, *Slavery in the Cities*, 28–31; Gould, " 'If I Can't Have My Rights,' " 188, 189.

9. Wade, *Slavery in the Cities*, 53–60; Goldfield, *Cotton Fields and Skyscrapers*, 48–49; Poesch and Bacot, *Louisiana Buildings*, 52; Gould, " 'If I Can't Have My Rights,' " 191–192. See also Virginia Meacham Gould, "The House That Was Never a Home: Slave Family and Household Organization, 1820–1850," *Slavery and Abolition* 18 (1997): 95.

10. Gross, *Double Character*, 98–99.

11. *Miller v. Belmonti* 1844.

12. Miller, "Refutation," 54–55; Searight, *New Orleans*, 111.

13. Jo-Ann Carrigan, *The Saffron Scourge: A History of Yellow Fever in Louisiana, 1791–1905* (Lafayette: University of Southwestern Louisiana Press, 1994), 138–39, 55; Duffy, *History of Medicine in Louisiana*, 1:356–57; Bennett Dowler, "Tableau of the Yellow Fever of 1853," in *Cohen's New Orleans Directory for 1854* (New Orleans: Office of the *Daily Picayune*, 1854), 15–16; Bennett Dowler, "Tableaux, Geographical, Commercial, Geological and Sanitary of New Orleans," in *Cohen's New Orleans and Lafayette Directory for 1852* (New Orleans: Office of the *Daily Delta*, 1852), 22–24. Little was known about the disease until the twentieth century. Yellow fever is an acute virus occurring mainly in the tropics and transmitted from person to person by the female *Aedes aegypti* mosquito. The mosquito uses artificial stagnant water to breed (for example, cisterns rather than swamps); thus, standing-water supplies on ships provide an ideal environment. Once a person has had yellow fever, she or he is immune, which is why strangers are more vulnerable than residents. The main symptom is a fever that can eventually cause jaundice (hence the name), damage to the body's vital organs, and even death, although most victims survive. Today there is still no cure, but most of those afflicted recover with rest and good nursing.

14. Carrigan, *Saffron Scourge*, 2, 4–11, 30, 42, 49; Henry Whipple, *Bishop Whipple's Southern Diary, 1843–44*, ed. Lester Shippee (1937; reprint, New York: DaCapo, 1968), 109, 117. The city suffered from other diseases that created a higher death toll, albeit fewer outbreaks, than yellow fever. In 1832, for example, cholera killed more than 5,000 people in New Orleans. In 1849, one-seventh of the city's population died in a cholera epidemic. See Carol Bleser, ed., *Tokens of Affection: Letters of a Planter's Daughter in the Old South* (Athens: University of Georgia Press, 1996), 138, 154; and Searight, *New Orleans*, 240.

15. Stampp, *Peculiar Institution*, 325. See also Eugene Genovese, *Roll, Jordan, Roll: The World the Slaves Made* (New York: Vintage, 1976), 7–12.

16. Reinders, "Slavery in New Orleans," 216, 219; Gould, " 'If I Can't Have My Rights,' " 190; Goldfield, *Cotton Fields and Skyscrapers*, 45–46; Miller, "Refutation," 53–54.

17. Jerah Johnson, "New Orleans' Congo Square: An Urban Setting for Early Afro-American Culture Formation," *Louisiana History* 32 (1991): 120–23,

136–39; Gary A. Donaldson, "A Window on Slave Culture: Dances at Congo Square in New Orleans, 1800–62," *Journal of Negro History* 69 (1984): 64.

18. Latrobe, *Journals*, 3:203–4.
19. Johnson, "New Orleans' Congo Square," 142–46; Latrobe, *Journals*, 3:203–4; [Paxton's] *New-Orleans Directory* (1822), excerpted in *DeBow's Review* 7 (July–December 1849): 419.
20. Wade, *Slavery in the Cities*, 82–85, 149–51; Goldfield, *Cotton Fields and Skyscrapers*, 50; Roger A. Fischer, "Racial Segregation in Antebellum New Orleans," *American Historical Review* 74 (February 1969): 933–34.
21. Frederick Law Olmsted, *The Cotton Kingdom* (1861; reprint, New York: Knopf, 1953), 234, 240–47.
22. Frederick Douglass, *Narrative of the Life of Frederick Douglass* (1845; reprint, New York: Signet, 1968), 50.
23. Carol Wilson, *Freedom at Risk: The Kidnapping of Free Blacks in America, 1780–1865* (Lexington: University Press of Kentucky, 1994).
24. *Miller v. Belmonti* 1844.
25. Ibid.; George Pollock was a lawyer and also held various posts, including positions with the New Orleans Navigation Company, the city's chamber of commerce, the Bank of the United States, and the Port of New Orleans. See Gaspard, "Rise of the Louisiana Bar," 193.
26. Michael Tadman, *Speculators and Slaves: Masters, Traders and Slaves in the Old South* (Madison: University of Wisconsin Press, 1989), 70; Frederic Bancroft, *Slave Trading in the Old South* (Baltimore: J. H. Furst, 1931), 315; Judith Kelleher Schafer, "New Orleans Slavery in 1850 As Seen in Advertisements," *Journal of Southern History* 47 (February 1981): 34; Richard Tansey, "Bernard Kendig and the New Orleans Slave Trade," *Louisiana History* 23 (1982): 159; Wade, *Slavery in the Cities*, 199.
27. Laurence J. Kotlikoff, "The Structure of Slave Prices in New Orleans, 1804–1862," *Economic Inquiry* 17 (1979): 497.
28. Schafer, "New Orleans Slavery in 1850," 33, 41.
29. Other Deep South markets opened in December. See Tadman, *Speculators and Slaves*, 70.
30. Herman Freudenberger and Jonathan B. Prichett, "The Domestic United States Slave Trade: New Evidence," *Journal of Interdisciplinary History* 21 (1991): 465.
31. Wade, *Slavery in the Cities*, 204; Reinders, "Slavery in New Orleans," 212; Bancroft, *Slave Trading in the Old South*, 318–20; Tansey, "Bernard Kendig," 160. For examples of how individual slave dealers operated, see Wendell Holmes Stephenson, *Isaac Franklin: Slave Trader and Planter of the Old South* (Baton Rouge: Louisiana State University Press, 1938).
32. Stampp, *Peculiar Institution*, 237–39; Bancroft, *Slave Trading in the Old South*, 312.
33. Joe Gray Taylor, *Negro Slavery in Louisiana* (Baton Rouge: Louisiana State University Press, 1963), 38–39; Tadman, *Speculators and Slaves*, 116, Kotlikoff, "Structure of Slave Prices," 498.

34. Factors, sometimes called commission merchants, bought and sold goods on behalf of a principal. They functioned as middlemen, taking a commission fee (usually 2.5 percent) whenever they sold a planter's crops or purchased supplies for him. The relationship between a planter and his factor was often highly personal. See Joseph Carlyle Sitterson, *Sugar Country: The Cane Sugar Industry in the South, 1753–1950* (Lexington: University Press of Kentucky, 1953), 185, 197, 201; and Richard Holcombe Kilbourne, Jr., *Louisiana's Commercial Law: The Antebellum Period* (Baton Rouge: Louisiana State University Press, 1980), 108–9.

35. *Miller v. Belmonti* 1844.

36. [Campbell's], *The Southern Business Directory and General Commercial Advertiser* (Charleston, S.C.: Walker and James, 1854), 157.

37. Edward T. Weeks, Sr., and Glenn R. Conrad, "Some Facts and Traditions about New Iberia," in *New Iberia: Essays on the Town and Its People*, 2d ed., comp. Glenn R. Conrad (Lafayette: University of Southwestern Louisiana, 1986), 49–59, 361–62; Conrad, *Dictionary of Louisiana Biography*, 1:570; Glenn R. Conrad, ed., *Land Records of the Attakapas District* (Lafayette: University of Southwestern Louisiana, 1990), 1:248, 267, 287; *Michel's New Orleans Register* (1833); *New-Orleans Directory* (1835); *Gibson's Guide and Directory to the State of Louisiana and the Cities of New Orleans and Lafayette* (New Orleans: John Gibson, 1838); Maurine Bergerie, *They Tasted Bayou Water: A Brief History of Iberia Parish* (New Orleans: Pelican, 1962), 30–31.

38. Roger Shugg, *Origins of Class Struggle in Louisiana: A Social History of White Farmers and Laborers During Slavery and After, 1840–75* (Baton Rouge: Louisiana State University Press, 1939), 6–7, 14; Grace King and John Ficklen, *A History of Louisiana*, 3d rev. ed. (New York: University Publishing, 1897), 201–2, 256, 262; Alton V. Moody, *Slavery on Louisiana Sugar Plantations* (1924; reprint, New York: AMS Press, 1976), 9–11; Starobin, *Industrial Slavery*, 41; Sitterson, *Sugar Country*, 25, 28; Baird, *View of the Valley*, 275. Solomon Northup provides a detailed first-person account of work on a sugar plantation in *Twelve Years a Slave*, ed. Sue Eakin and Joseph Logsdon (1853; reprint, Baton Rouge: Louisiana State University Press, 1968), 159–63.

39. Conrad, "Wilderness Paradise," 53–57; Carl A. Brasseaux, "Entertainment, Sports, and Recreation in New Iberia, 1830–1978," in *New Iberia: Essays on the Town and Its People*, 2d ed., comp. Glenn R. Conrad (Lafayette: University of Southwestern Louisiana, 1986), 464; Sitterson, *Sugar Country*, 76–80; Bergerie, *They Tasted Bayou Water*, 65, 89. Pine Island is now known as Jefferson Island, after the actor Joseph Jefferson, who bought it in 1870. Both Jefferson Island and Shadows-on-the-Teche are today popular tourist attractions.

40. Dale A. Somers, *The Rise of Sports in New Orleans, 1850–1900* (Baton Rouge: Louisiana State University Press, 1972), 23–30; Sitterson, *Sugar Country*, 76–80.

41. *Miller v. Belmonti* 1844. The bankruptcy hearing was not Miller's only legal action that year. The State Supreme Court, sitting at Opelousas in September 1841, heard the case of *Miller v. Lelen*, an appeal from the Fifth District Court

for St. Martin Parish. Miller was suing a neighbor for trespass. See *Miller v. Lelen*, 19 La. 331 (Opelousas, September 1841).

42. Edward J. Balleisen, *Navigating Failure: Bankruptcy and Commercial Society in Antebellum America* (Chapel Hill: University of North Carolina Press, 2001) 5, 27, 31–34; Kilbourne, *Louisiana's Commercial Law*, 121, 157–58; Sitterson, *Sugar Country*, 177, 201; William J. Cooper, Jr., *The South and the Politics of Slavery, 1828–56* (Baton Rouge: Louisiana State University Press, 1978), 100–101; Anonymous, *Biographical and Historical Memoirs*, 1:188; Merl E. Reed, "Boom or Bust: Louisiana's Economy During the 1830s," *Louisiana History* 4 (winter 1963): 49–50.

43. *Joachim Kohn and Others v. John F. Miller and Another, Syndics of the Creditors of said John F. Miller, an Insolvent*, 5 Rob. 515 (Opelousas, September 1843).

CHAPTER 6   *Sally and Louis Belmonti*

1. *Gibson's Guide and Directory*; [Michel's] *New Orleans Directory and Register* (New Orleans: J. L. Sollée, 1841); *New Orleans Directory for 1842* (New Orleans: Pitts and Clarke, 1842). Belmonti's name does not appear in any extant directory after this time, although there is a listing for an "L. Bellmonte, fmc [free man of color]" at 285 Marais Street in the 1857 *Mygatt and Co.'s Directory*. Nowhere else in the record is there mention of Belmonti's being other than white.

2. Henry C. Castellanos, *New Orleans As It Was: Episodes of Louisiana Life* (1905; reprint, Baton Rouge: Louisiana State University Press, 1978), 217–18; Tregle, *Louisiana in the Age of Jackson*, 20–21; John H. B. Latrobe, *Southern Travels: Journals of John H. B. Latrobe*, ed. Samuel Wilson, Jr. (1834; reprint, New Orleans: Historic New Orleans Collection, 1986), 150; Whipple, *Diary*, 111.

3. The term *Creole* is used here to mean people born in Louisiana of French or Spanish ancestry.

4. Crété, *Daily Life in Louisiana*, 36; Dominguez, *White by Definition*, 118; Wade, *Slavery in the Cities*, 5; Toledano, *National Trust Guide to New Orleans*, 48–50.

5. Tregle, *Louisiana in the Age of Jackson*, 14; Rousey, *Policing the Southern City*, 37; Whipple, *Diary*, 100.

6. *Miller v. Belmonti* 1844. The testimony of A. Piernas is not in the original court record but is reprinted in Miller, "Refutation."

7. Castellanos, *New Orleans As It Was*, 217–18; *Miller v. Belmonti* 1844; Miller, "Refutation," 21. The bill of sale to Belmonti lists Charles as being four years old in July 1838. Sarah Canby put Charles's age in December 1845 at eleven, placing his birthdate in 1834. Yet when Canby sold Sally and her children back to John Miller in December 1834, the records make no mention of Charles. Perhaps he had not been born yet or, as a newborn, was omitted from the list.

8. Miller, "Refutation," 21–22.

9. Schafer, *Slavery, the Civil Law and the Supreme Court of Louisiana*, 181–82.

10. *Miller v. Belmonti* 1844.

11. *U.S. Census*, Louisiana, 1840.

12. *Miller v. Belmonti* 1844.

13. Ibid. Speaking German was not necessarily inconsistent with slave status. The *New Orleans Bee* (14 February 1850) ran an advertisement to recover a mulatto fugitive slave who spoke English, French, and German.

14. Kohn was also a banker who financed several buildings in the 1830s that are still standing today at 916–24 Royal Street. See Stanley Clisby Arthur, *Old New Orleans* (Gretna, La.: Pelican, 1990), 92.

15. Advertisement for E. Johns and Company, *Michel & Co. New-Orleans Annual and Commercial Directory, for 1843* (New Orleans: J. L. Sollée, 1842); Conrad, *Dictionary of Louisiana Biography*, 1:436; John H. Baron, "Paul Emile Johns of New Orleans: Tycoon, Musician, and Friend of Chopin," in *Report of the Eleventh Congress* [of the International Musicological Society] (Copenhagen, 1972), 246–50.

16. Tregle, *Louisiana in the Age of Jackson*, 14; Anonymous, *Biographical and Historical Memoirs*, 1:184; Crété, *Daily Life in Louisiana*, 42; Carla Downer Pritchett, "Case Law Reporters in Nineteenth Century Louisiana," in *A Law Unto Itself? Essays in the New Louisiana Legal History*, ed. Warren M. Billings and Mark F. Fernandez (Baton Rouge: Louisiana State University Press, 2001), 64, 72.

17. *Miller v. Belmonti* 1844; Miller, "Refutation," 55–56.

18. *Miller v. Belmonti* 1844.

19. Vincent Nolte, *Fifty Years in Both Hemispheres; or Reminiscences of a Former Merchant* (1854; reprint, New York: Redfield, 1934), 318; Anonymous, *Biographical and Historical Memoirs*, 1:182–83. For more on Lafayette's visit, see his secretary's account of the trip in A. Levasseur, *Lafayette in America in 1824 and 1825*, trans. John D. Godman (Philadelphia: Carey and Lea, 1829).

20. *Miller v. Belmonti* 1844.

21. Catherine Clinton, " 'Southern Dishonor': Flesh, Blood, Race, and Bondage," in *In Joy and in Sorrow: Women, Family, and Marriage in the Victorian South, 1830–1900*, ed. Carol Bleser (New York: Oxford University Press, 1991), 56–58; John W. Blassingame, *The Slave Community: Plantation Life in the Antebellum South*, rev. and enlarged ed. (New York: Oxford University Press, 1978), 154–55; John W. Blassingame, *Black New Orleans: 1860–80* (Chicago: University of Chicago Press, 1973), 17, 201.

22. Wade, *Slavery in the Cities*, 121–24; David C. Rankin, "The Tannenbaum Thesis Reconsidered: Slavery and Race Relations in Antebellum Louisiana," *Southern Studies* 18 (spring 1979): 21–22; Carl A. Brasseaux, Keith P. Fontenot, and Claude F. Oubre, *Creoles of Color in the Bayou Country* (Jackson: University of Mississippi Press, 1994), 8.

23. *Miller v. Belmonti* 1844.

24. Miller, "Refutation," 21; Schwartz, *Born in Bondage*, 178–79.

25. Steven E. Brown, "Sexuality and the Slave Community," *Phylon* 42 (spring 1981): 3; Blassingame, *Slave Community*, 149–53, 158–61, 165–70; Taylor, *Negro Slavery in Louisiana*, 123; Deborah Gray White, *Arn't I a Woman? Female Slaves in the Plantation South* (New York: Norton, 1985), 97; James

Trussell and Richard Steckel, "The Age of Slaves at Menarche and Their First Birth," *Journal of Interdisciplinary History* 8 (winter 1978): 504.

26. *Daily Picayune*, 2 September 1846; Charles Mackay, *Life and Liberty in America; or Sketches of a Tour in the United States and Canada, in 1857–8* (New York: Harper, 1859), 316–18; Alex[ander] Mackay, *The Western World; or Travels in the United States in 1846–47*, 2d ed. (1849; reprint, New York: Negro Universities Press, 1968), 300–301; Whipple, *Diary*, 114.

27. Miller, "Refutation," 55–56; *Miller v. Belmonti* 1844.

28. *Cohen's New Orleans Directory for 1855* (New Orleans: Office of the *Daily Picayune*, 1855); Conrad, *Dictionary of Louisiana Biography*, 1:511.

29. *Miller v. Belmonti* 1844.

30. *Daily Picayune*, 9 April 1844, 25 May 1844, 31 May 1844.

CHAPTER 7   *From Black to White*

1. Buchanan later served a justice of the State Supreme Court, from 1853 to 1862. William Kernan Dart, "The Justices of the Supreme Court," *Louisiana Historical Quarterly* 4 (January 1921): 118.

2. *Miller v. Belmonti* 1844.

3. Ibid.

4. Ibid.

5. Ibid.

6. Shafer, *Slavery, the Civil Law, and the Supreme Court of Louisiana*, 270.

7. *Miller v. Belmonti* 1845. Printed briefs began appearing in the 1820s, but until 1877 attorneys had the option of providing handwritten or printed ones. Upton's brief in this appeal was printed. See Florence M. Jumonville, " 'The People's Friend, the Tyrant's Foe': Law-Related New Orleans Imprints, 1803–60," in *A Law Unto Itself? Essays in the New Louisiana Legal History*, ed. Warren M. Billings and Mark F. Fernandez (Baton Rouge: Louisiana State University Press, 2001), 56.

8. *Miller v. Belmonti* 1845.

9. Ibid.

10. Ibid.

11. Ibid.; *Miller v. Belmonti* 1844.

12. *Miller v. Belmonti* 1845; *Miller v. Belmonti* 1844. The case was mentioned in the *Daily Picayune* on at least seven occasions up to this point.

13. *Miller v. Belmonti* 1845.

14. Ibid.

15. Schafer, *Slavery, the Civil Law, and the Supreme Court of Louisiana*, xii; Warren M. Billings, ed., *Historic Rules of the Supreme Court of Louisiana, 1813–79* (Lafayette: University of Southwestern Louisiana Press, 1985), xi, xvi.

16. Conrad, *Dictionary of Louisiana Biography*, 1:551; Henry A. Bullard, "A Discourse on the Life, Character and Writings of François-Xavier Martin," in *Historical Collections of Louisiana*, ed. B. F. French (Philadelphia: Daniels and Smith, 1850), 2:17–40; Anonymous, *Biographical and Historical Memoirs*,

1:83; Schafer, *Slavery, the Civil Law and the Supreme Court of Louisiana*, 223; Mark F. Fernandez, "From Chaos to Continuity: Early Reforms of the Supreme Court of Louisiana, 1845–52," *Louisiana History* 28 (1987): 7; Jumonville, "People's Friend," 52–53.

17. Fernandez, "From Chaos to Continuity," 21–26; Henry Plauché Dart, "The History of the Supreme Court of Louisiana," *Louisiana Historical Quarterly* 4 (1921): 35; Billings, *Historic Rules*, xiv.

18. Letter from Henry A. Bullard to Josiah Stoddard Johnston (2 February 1822), in correspondence of Josiah Stoddard Johnston, Historical Society of Pennsylvania, Philadelphia, reprinted in Richard Holcombe Kilbourne, Jr., *A History of the Louisiana Civil Code, 1803–1839* (Baton Rouge: Louisiana State University Press, 1987), 98–99.

19. Conrad, *Dictionary of Louisiana Biography*, 1127; "The Late Henry Adams Bullard," *DeBow's Review* 12 (January 1852): 50–56; "Memoir of Hon. Henry Adams Bullard, LL.D.," in *Historical Collections of Louisiana*, ed. B. F. French (New York: D. Appleton, 1851), 3:5–8; Bullard and Curry, *New Digest of the Statutes of the State of Louisiana*, 1.

20. Dart, "Justices of the Supreme Court," 117; Conrad, *Dictionary of Louisiana Biography*, 2:743.

21. Fernandez, "From Chaos to Continuity," 26–28; Dora J. Bonquois, "The Career of Henry Adams Bullard, Louisiana Jurist, Legislator, and Educator," *Louisiana Historical Quarterly* 23 (October 1940): 1035; Conrad, *Dictionary of Louisiana Biography*, 1:335; William E. Wiethoff, *A Peculiar Humanism: The Judicial Advocacy of Slavery in the High Courts of the Old South, 1820–1850* (Athens: University of Georgia Press, 1996), 149–50.

22. *Adelle v. Beauregard*, I Mart. La. 183 (fall 1810); Schafer, *Slavery, the Civil Law, and the Supreme Court of Louisiana*, 20.

23. *Miller v. Belmonti* 1845. It was not unusual for judges to forgo physical examination of plaintiffs. In her analysis of sixty-eight racial identity cases in the antebellum South, Ariela Gross found that only twenty mentioned examination of the plaintiff's body. The use of witnesses' descriptions was more common. See Ariela J. Gross, "Litigating Whiteness: Trials of Racial Determination in the Nineteenth Century South," *Yale Law Journal* 108 (1998): 138–39.

24. *Miller v. Belmonti* 1845; Ingersoll, *Mammon and Manon in Early New Orleans*, 263–64; Schafer, *Slavery, the Civil Law, and the Supreme Court of Louisiana*, 17–19. Owners could and did sell couples apart and parents from children. In some states, among them Louisiana, the sale of young children from their mothers was illegal; but this provision was routinely ignored.

25. *Miller v. Belmonti* 1845; *Sally Miller v. Louis Belmonti*, 11 Rob. 339 (New Orleans, July 1845). The result was not surprising. The Louisiana Supreme Court heard freedom suits throughout the antebellum era. According to Schafer, "The Court was generally in favor of freedom—at least until the act of 1857 prohibited emancipation—as long as the slave could prove he or she was entitled to it." See Schafer, *Slavery, the Civil Law, and the Supreme Court of Louisiana*, 220—21

26. Samuel and Samuel, *Great Days of the Garden District*, 4, 23.

27. *New Orleans Tropic*, 30 June 1845, reprinted in *National Anti-Slavery Standard*, 31 July 1845; *Jeffersonian Republican* (New Orleans), 24 June 1845.
28. Trial transcript, *John F. Miller v. Sally Miller*, no. 24,454, Fifth District Court of Louisiana, 17 May 1848, Supreme Court of Louisiana Collection, Earl K. Long Library, University of New Orleans (hereafter referred to as *Miller v. Miller* 1848).

CHAPTER 8   *White Slavery*

1. Thomas R. R. Cobb, *An Inquiry into the Law of Negro Slavery in the United States of America* (Philadelphia: T. and J. W. Johnson, 1858), 2:66–67.
2. *Mobile Register*, 8 January 1859.
3. Thomas D. Morris, *Southern Slavery and the Law, 1619–1860* (Chapel Hill: University of North Carolina Press, 1996), 21–22.
4. Ibid., 24–25; Joel Williamson, *New People: Miscegenation in the United States* (Baton Rouge: Louisiana State University Press, 1995), 8.
5. Winthrop D. Jordan, *White Over Black: American Attitudes toward the Negro, 1550–1812* (Chapel Hill: University of North Carolina Press, 1968), 167–71; Morris, *Southern Slavery and the Law*, 21–29; Stampp, *Peculiar Institution*, 193–95; Williamson, *New People*, 3, 13–15; Ira Berlin, *Slaves Without Masters: The Free Negro in the Antebellum South* (New York: Pantheon, 1974), 97–99, 161–63; Carl N. Degler, *Neither White Nor Black: Slavery and Race Relations in Brazil and the United States* (New York: Macmillan, 1971), 101.
6. Blassingame, *Black New Orleans*, 17; Schafer, "New Orleans Slavery in 1850 As Seen in Advertisements," 50; Ingersoll, *Mammon and Manon in Early New Orleans*, 333–37.
7. Solomon Northup, *Twelve Years a Slave*, ed. Sue Eakin and Joseph Logsdon (1853; reprint, Baton Rouge: Louisiana State University Press, 1968), 186.
8. *Sally Miller v. Louis Belmonti*.
9. Ibid. See also *Adelle v. Beauregard*, I Mart. La. 183 (fall 1810). The judge's use of the term *person of color* had a connotation more specific than it does in modern usage. Today it is frequently used to describe any person not of wholly European extraction; the terms *black* and *person of color* are sometimes used interchangeably. In antebellum Louisiana, however, the term was used more specifically to distinguish people of mixed racial ancestry from blacks or Africans. People of color (mulattos) were presumed to be free unless proven otherwise; blacks were not.
10. Frederick Douglass, *My Bondage and My Freedom*, ed. William L. Andrews (1855; reprint, Urbana: University of Illinois Press, 1987), 60.
11. F. James Davis, *Who Is Black? One Nation's Definition* (State College: Pennsylvania State University Press, 1991), 20–23, 29–30. See also Paul Spickard and G. Reginald Daniel, eds., *Racial Thinking in the United States: Uncompleted Independence* (Notre Dame, Ind.: University of Notre Dame Press, 2004); Laura Newell Morris, *Human Populations: Genetic Variation and Evolution* (San Francisco: Chandler, 1971); Richard H. Osborne, ed., *The Biological and Social Meaning of Race* (San Francisco: Freeman, 1971); and

Ashley Montagu, *Man's Most Dangerous Myth: The Fallacy of Race*, rev. ed. (New York: Harcourt Brace Jovanovich, 1964).

12. Williamson, *New People*, chap. 1. See also George M. Frederickson, *White Supremacy: A Comparative Study in American and South African History* (New York: Oxford University Press, 1995); and Ronald Takaki, *Iron Cages: Race and Culture in Nineteenth Century America* (New York: Knopf, 1979).

13. William Jay, "Condition of the Free People of Color," in *The Free People of Color* (1838; reprint, New York: Arno Press and the *New York Times*, 1969), 391.

14. *National Anti-Slavery Standard*, 20 October 1842.

15. William Wells Brown, *Narrative of William Wells Brown*, in *Five Slave Narratives*, ed. William Loren Katz (1847; reprint, New York: Arno Press and the *New York Times*, 1969), 61–62.

16. *National Anti-Slavery Standard*, 3 October 1850. In addition to those cases of slaves who were white, numerous cases exist of persons whose physical appearance was white but whose heritage was in doubt or unknown. See B. A. Botkin, ed., *Lay My Burden Down: A Folk History of Slavery* (1945; reprint, Athens: University of Georgia Press, 1973), 159–60; Charles Perdue, Jr., Thomas E. Barden, and Robert K. Phillips, eds., *Weevils in the Wheat: Interviews with Virginia Ex-Slaves* (Charlottesville: University of Virginia Press, 1976), 79; Mackay, *Life and Liberty in America*, 199–201; and Lawrence R. Tenzer, *The Forgotten Cause of the Civil War: A New Look at the Slavery Issue* (Manahawkin, N.J.: Scholars' Publishing House, 1997), 23–38.

17. C. Peter Ripley and Jeffrey S. Rossbach, eds., *The Black Abolitionist Papers*, vol. 1, *The British Isles, 1830–1865* (Chapel Hill: University of North Carolina Press, 1985), 203; William Craft, *Running a Thousand Miles for Freedom, or the Escape of William and Ellen Craft from Slavery* (1860; reprint, Baton Rouge: Louisiana State University Press, 1999), 4–6; *Liberator*, 5 September 1835.

18. Letter from Parker Pillsbury to William Lloyd Garrison, *National Anti-Slavery Standard*, 12 November 1853; Craft, *Running a Thousand Miles for Freedom*, 4–6; William Chambers, *American Slavery and Colour* (1857; reprint, New York: Negro Universities Press, 1968), 3.

19. Julie Winch, "Philadelphia and the Other Underground Railroad," *Pennsylvania Magazine of History and Biography* 61 (January 1987): 23.

20. Ira Berlin, *Many Thousands Gone: The First Two Centuries of Slavery in North America* (Cambridge, Mass.: Belknap Press of Harvard University Press, 1998), 1.

21. Several recent autobiographies aptly reveal the results of continuing to force people into unworkable racial categorizations. For example, see Gregory Howard Williams, *Life on the Color Line: The True Story of a White Boy Who Discovered He Was Black* (New York: Dutton, 1995); Shirlee Taylor Haizlip, *The Sweeter the Juice: A Family Memoir in Black and White* (New York: Touchstone, 1994); and Pauli Murray, *Proud Shoes: The Story of an American Family* (New York: Harper and Row, 1984). See also James M. O'Toole, *Passing for White: Race, Religion, and the Healy Family, 1820–1920* (Amherst: University of Massachusetts Press, 2002).

CHAPTER 9 *Sally Miller and Salomé Muller*

1. "Sally Miller" (New Orleans: Office of the *New Orleans Tropic*, 1845), copy in the collection of the New York Public Library; *New Orleans Tropic*, 30 June 1845, reprinted in *National Anti-Slavery Standard*, 31 July 1845.
2. "Sally Miller," 1–17.
3. Ibid., 17–24. The *Picayune* found amusement in the pamphlet's publication: "Sallied down Camp Street, and was met by a hard-faced little urchin, who asked us to buy 'sally muller'—remembered that the Supreme Court have decided that Sally Muller is free and to be neither bought nor sold, and so did not comply with the request of the little *litterateur*." See *Daily Picayune*, 25 July 1845.
4. Gross, *Double Character*, 16.
5. Trial transcript, *Salomé Muller v. John F. Miller and Sarah Canby*, no. 1,403, U.S. Circuit Court, Fifth District of Louisiana, 1845–46, National Archives, Southwest Branch, Fort Worth, Tex., copy (hereafter referred to as *Muller v. Miller and Canby* 1845–46).
6. Ibid.
7. Ibid.
8. Ibid.
9. *Miller v. Belmonti* 1845.
10. Miller, "Refutation," 3.
11. Ibid., 9–10, 22.
12. Ibid., 9.
13. Ibid., 10.
14. Ibid., 32–33. Wheeler's testimony is missing from the original trial record but can be found in the reprint of the trial record in Miller's pamphlet.
15. *Miller v. Belmonti* 1845.
16. Miller, "Refutation," 7. The baptismal certificate for "Jean . . . fils naturel de Marie, quarteronne, esclave John Miller" is not in the original trial records but is reprinted in ibid., 58.
17. Ibid., 14, 21–22.
18. Ibid., 15.
19. Ibid., 16–19.
20. *Miller v. Miller* 1848.
21. Ibid.
22. Ibid.
23. Ibid.
24. Ibid.
25. Ibid.
26. Ibid.
27. Ibid.
28. Ibid.
29. Ibid.
30. Ibid.
31. Ibid.

32. The Wilsons had apparently moved from Alabama to Mississippi between 1810 and 1818.
33. *Muller v. Miller and Canby* 1845–46.
34. Ibid; Schwartz, *Born in Bondage*, 156–58.
35. *Muller v. Miller and Canby* 1845–46.
36. Ibid.
37. *Miller v. Miller* 1848.
38. Ibid; Kendall, "Shadow Over the City," 158–59.
39. *Miller v. Miller* 1848.
40. Ibid.
41. Ibid.
42. Preston would soon become a Supreme Court judge himself. Born in Virginia, he had served in the War of 1812 and in 1845 had been a member of the Louisiana state constitutional convention. He served on the Court from 1850 until 1852, when he was killed in a steamboat accident on Lake Ponchartrain. See Dart, "Justices of the Supreme Court," 118.
43. *Miller v. Miller* 1848.
44. Ibid.
45. *Miller v. Miller* 1849.
46. Ibid.
47. Ibid.
48. Ibid.
49. During the Civil War, Rost served as commissioner to France and Spain.
50. Fernandez, "From Chaos to Continuity," 21, 28–30; Conrad, *Dictionary of Louisiana Biography*, 1:290, 465; 2:697, 747; Dart, "Justices of the Supreme Court," 116–118; Dart, "History of the Supreme Court of Louisiana," 38–44.
51. *Miller v. Miller* 1849.
52. Schafer, *Slavery, the Civil Law, and the Supreme Court of Louisiana*, 275–76.
53. *Miller v. Miller* 1849; *Miller v. Miller.* 4 La. Ann. 354 (1849).
54. *Miller v. Miller* 1849.
55. *Miller v. Belmonti* 1844.
56. Edward L. Ayers, *Vengeance and Justice: Crime and Punishment in the Nineteenth-Century American South* (New York: Oxford, 1974), 13.
57. *Daily Picayune*, 31 May 1844.
58. *Miller v. Miller* 1849.
59. Ibid.

Conclusion

1. *Miller v. Belmonti* 1844.
2. Ibid.
3. *Miller v. Belmonti* 1845.
4. Miller, "Refutation," 4–6.
5. *Miller v. Belmonti* 1845.

6. Walter S. Johnson, "The Slave Trader, the White Slave, and the Politics of Racial Determination in the 1850s," *Journal of American History* 87 (June 2000): 22; Gross, "Litigating Whiteness," 109.

7. *Muller v. Miller and Canby* 1845–46.

8. *Miller v. Belmonti* 1844.

9. "Sally Miller," 7–8.

10. An advertisement from the *New Orleans Bee* (31 May 1850) for the fugitive slave Aimie demonstrated that residents there found nothing inconsistent about a slave resembling a person of German origin. Aimie was described as a "quarteroon" with "the appearance of a German girl."

11. *Miller v. Belmonti* 1844.

12. Williamson, *New People*, 18–19.

13. *Miller v. Belmonti* 1845.

14. Ibid.

15. Gross, "Litigating Whiteness," 156–57.

16. Miller, "Refutation," 21.

17. *Miller v. Belmonti* 1844.

18. Gross, "Litigating Whiteness," 167–68.

19. Ibid., 176.

20. *Daily Picayune*, 25 May 1844.

21. Gross, "Litigating Whiteness," 111–18, 132; Teresa Zackodnik, "Fixing the Color Line: The Mulatto, Southern Courts, and Racial Identity," *American Quarterly* 53 (September 2001): 422–23.

22. Gross, "Litigating Whiteness," 176.

23. Ibid.; Blassingame, *Black New Orleans*, 201. Richard Kluger has called Louisiana "a racial bouillabaisse unlike any other"; see his *Simple Justice* (New York: Knopf, 1975), 75.

24. Olmsted, *Cotton Kingdom*, 228–29.

25. Latrobe, *Journals*, 3:183.

26. *Miller v. Belmonti* 1844.

27. Miller, "Refutation," 3.

28. *Daily Picayune*, 9 April 1844, 26 June 1844.

29. *Pennsylvania Freeman*, 25 April 1844, 3 July 1845. The case was also mentioned in *National Anti-Slavery Standard*, 6 June 1844, 14 July 1845, 31 July 1845; and *Anti-Slavery Bugle*, 25 July 1845.

30. Mary Niall Mitchell, "'Rosebloom and Pure White,' or So It Seemed," *American Quarterly* 54 (September 2002): 369–80, 388.

31. William L. Andrews, introduction, in Andrews, ed., *From Fugitive Slave to Free Man: The Autobiographies of William Wells Brown* (New York: Mentor, 1993), 3–4.

32. William Wells Brown, *Clotel* (1853), in *Three Classic African-American Novels*, ed. William L. Andrews (New York: Penguin, 1990), 189–92.

33. William E. Farrison, *William Wells Brown: Author and Reformer* (Chicago: University of Chicago Press, 1969), 222.

34. Craft, *Running a Thousand Miles for Freedom*, 4–5. For a literary analysis of Craft's use of Sally's story, see Lindon Barrett, "Hand-Writing: Legibility and

the White Body in *Running a Thousand Miles for Freedom*," *American Literature* 69 (June 1997): 320–22.

35. Conrad, *Dictionary of Louisiana Biography*, 1:138; John Cleman, *George Washington Cable Revisited* (New York: Twayne, 1996), 1–19; Louis D. Rubin, *George W. Cable: The Life and Times of a Southern Heretic* (New York: Pegasus, 1969), 67.

36. George Washington Cable, "Salome Müller, The White Slave," in Cable, *Strange True Stories of Louisiana* (New York: Scribner's, 1889), 145–91; also published as Cable, "Salome Müller, The White Slave," *Century Magazine* 38 (May 1889): 56–69. For literary analysis of the article, see Cleman, *George Washington Cable Revisited*, 139–41; and Alice Hall Petry, "The Limits of Truth in Cable's 'Salome Müller,' " *Papers on Language and Literature* 27 (winter 1991): 20–31.

37. Cable, "How I Got Them," in *Strange True Stories of Louisiana*, 2–4.

38. Cleman, *George Washington Cable Revisited*, 1.

39. Deiler, "System of Redemption," 426–47; Louis Voss, "Sally Mueller, The German Slave," *Louisiana Historical Quarterly* (1929): 447–60.

40. Berchtold, "Decline of German Ethnicity in New Orleans," 11–12.

41. Voss, "Sally Mueller."

42. Kendall, "Shadow Over the City," 142–65. My first account of the case, based on the transcripts from the first trial and appeal, supported Sally's claim. See Carol Wilson, "Sally Miller, the White Slave," *Louisiana History* 40 (spring 1999): 133–53.

43. John Bailey, *The Lost German Slave Girl* (Sydney, Australia: Macmillan, 2003).

44. *Morrison v. White*. 16 La. Ann. 100 (New Orleans, February 1861); Johnson, "Slave Trader," 13, 28–29, 35; Gross, "Litigating Whiteness," 172–75.

45. *Morrison v. White*; Johnson, "Slave Trader," 15, 20, 27, 32, 37; Gross, "Litigating Whiteness," 175–76.

46. *Morrison v. White*; Johnson, "Slave Trader," 36; Gross, "Litigating Whiteness," 175–76. For the similar case of Abby Guy in Arkansas, see Zackodnik, "Fixing the Color Line," 420–52; and Robert S. Shafer, "White Persons Held to Racial Slavery in Antebellum Arkansas," *Arkansas Historical Quarterly* 44 (summer 1985): 134–55.

47. Gross, "Litigating Whiteness," 166, 176.

48. Thomas F. Harwood, "The Abolitionist Image of Louisiana and Mississippi," *Louisiana History* 7 (fall 1966): 281–303.

49. Judith Kelleher Schafer, *Becoming Free, Remaining Free: Manumission and Enslavement in New Orleans, 1846–1852* (Baton Rouge: Louisiana State University Press, 2003), 12, 14, 71, 73, 81, 89.

50. Gross, *Slavery in the Courtroom*, 67; Williamson, *New People*, 65.

51. Carl A. Brasseaux, *The Courthouses of Louisiana* (Lafayette: University of Southwestern Louisiana Press, 1977), 153

52. *François Duplessis et al. v. John F. Miller*. 6 La. Ann. 683 (Opelousas, September 1851). The case was decided in September 1850 but was not reported until the following year.

53. Conrad, *Dictionary of Louisiana Biography*, 1:570

54. *Harvey Beach v. Miller's Testamentary Executors et al.* 15 La. Ann. 601 (Opelousas, August 1860).

55. Conrad, "Wilderness Paradise," 57.

56. Conrad, *Dictionary of Louisiana Biography*, 1:329–30; Weeks and Conrad, "Some Facts and Traditions about New Iberia," 50–51; Elizabeth Urban Alexander, *Notorious Woman: The Celebrated Case of Myra Clark Gaines* (Baton Rouge: Louisiana State University Press, 2001), 1–4.

57. *Miller v. Miller* 1848.

58. Cable, "Salome Müller," *Century Magazine*, 69.

59. Voss, "Sally Mueller," 260. My search of the 1850 and 1860 Sacramento, California, census for the names Sally or Salomé Miller or Muller, Frederick King, and John Given turned up no evidence.

60. White, *Aren't I a Woman?*, 24.

BIBLIOGRAPHY

Primary Sources

COURT RECORDS

Trial transcript, *Sally Miller v. Louis Belmonti and John F. Miller* (called in warranty), no. 23,041, First District Court of Louisiana, 24 January–25 June 1844. Supreme Court of Louisiana Collection, Earl K. Long Library, University of New Orleans.

Trial transcript, *Sally Miller v. Louis Belmonti and John F. Miller* (called in warranty), no. 5,623 Supreme Court of Louisiana, 13 July 1844–30 June 1845. Supreme Court of Louisiana Collection, Earl K. Long Library, University of New Orleans.

Trial transcript, *John F. Miller v. Sally Miller*, no. 24,454, Fifth District Court of Louisiana, 17 December 1845–17 May 1848. Supreme Court of Louisiana Collection, Earl K. Long Library, University of New Orleans.

Trial transcript, *John F. Miller v. Sally Miller*, no. 1114, Supreme Court of Louisiana, 14 June 1848–21 May 1849. Supreme Court of Louisiana Collection, Earl K. Long Library, University of New Orleans.

Trial transcript, *Salomé Muller v. John F. Miller and Sarah Canby*, no. 1,403, U.S. Circuit Court, Fifth District of Louisiana, 25 June 1845–22 May 1846. National Archives Southwest Branch, Fort Worth, Tex. Copy.

PUBLISHED CASE REPORTS

Adelle v. Beauregard. I Mart. La. 183 (fall 1810).

François Duplessis et al. v. John F. Miller. 6 La. Ann. 683 (Opelousas, September 1851).

Harvey Beach v. Miller's Testamentary Executors et al. 15 La. Ann. 601. (Opelousas, August 1860).

Joachim Kohn and Others v. John F. Miller and Another, Syndics of the Creditors of said John F. Miller, an Insolvent. 5 Rob. 515 (Opelousas, September 1843).

Miller v. Lelen. 19 La. 331 (Opelousas, September 1841).

Miller v. Miller. 4 La. Ann. 354 (1849).

Morrison v. White. 16 La. Ann. 100 (New Orleans, February 1861).

Sally Miller v. Louis Belmonti. 11 Rob. 339 (New Orleans, July 1845).

NEWSPAPERS

American Watchman (Wilmington, Del.), 7 January 1818.

Anti-Slavery Bugle, 25 July 1845.

Daily Picayune, 9 April 1844, 25 May 1844, 31 May 1844, 26 June 1844, 25 July 1845, 2 September 1846.

DeBow's Review 7 (July–December 1849).

Jeffersonian Republican (New Orleans), 24 June 1845.

L'ami des lois (New Orleans), 7 March 1818.

Liberator, 5 September 1835.

Louisiana Gazette, 5–14 March 1818.

Mobile Register, 8 January 1859.

National Anti-Slavery Standard, 20 October 1842, 6 June 1844, 14 July 1845, 31 July 1845, 3 October 1850, 12 November 1853.

New Orleans Bee, 14 February 1850, 31 May 1850.

Niles' Register, 1 November 1817, 31 January 1818, 11 April 1818, 2 May 1818.

Pennsylvania Freeman, 25 April 1844, 3 July 1845.

TRAVELERS' ACCOUNTS

Baird, Robert. *View of the Valley of the Mississippi.* 2d ed. Philadelphia: H. S. Tanner, 1834.

Brackenridge, Henry. *Views of Louisiana.* Pittsburgh: Cramer, Spear, and Eichbaum, 1814.

Darby, William. *A Geographical Description of the State of Louisiana.* Philadelphia: John Melish, 1816.

Evans, Estwick. "A Pedestrious Tour, of Four Thousand Miles Through the Western States and Territories During the Winter and Spring of 1818." In *Early Western Travels, 1748–1846,* volume 8, edited by Reuben G. Thwaites, 325–64. 1819. Reprint, Cleveland: Arthur H. Clark, 1904.

Flint, Timothy. *Recollections of the Last Ten Years in the Valley of the Mississippi,* edited by George R. Brooks. 1826. Reprint, Carbondale: Southern Illinois University Press, 1968.

Flügel, J. G. "Pages from a Journal of a Voyage down the Mississippi to New Orleans in 1817," edited by Felix Flugel. *Louisiana Historical Quarterly* 7 (1924): 414–40.

Hall, A. Oakley. *The Manhattaner in New Orleans.* 1847. Reprint, Baton Rouge: Louisiana State University Press, 1976.

Latrobe, Benjamin Henry. *The Journals of Benjamin Henry Latrobe, 1799–1820, From Philadelphia to New Orleans,* volume 3, edited by Edward C. Carter III, John C. Van Horne, and Lee W. Formwalt. New Haven: Yale University Press, 1980.

Latrobe, John H. B. *Southern Travels: Journal of John H. B. Latrobe,* edited by Samuel Wilson, Jr. 1834. New Orleans: Historical New Orleans Collection, 1986.

Levasseur, A. *Lafayette in America in 1824 and 1825*, translated by John D. Godman. Philadelphia: Carey and Lea, 1829.

Mackay, Alex[ander]. *The Western World; or Travels in the United States in 1846–47*, 2d edition. 1849. Reprint, New York: Negro Universities Press, 1968.

Mackay, Charles. *Life and Liberty in America: or Sketches of a Tour in the United States and Canada, in 1857–8*. New York: Harper, 1859.

Nolte, Vincent. *Fifty Years in Both Hemispheres; or Reminiscences of a Former Merchant*. 1854. Reprint, New York: Redfield, 1934.

Paul Wilhelm, Duke of Württemberg. *Travels in North America, 1822–24*, edited by R. Nitske and S. Lottinville. Norman: University of Oklahoma Press, 1973.

Sealsfield, Charles [Karl Pöstl]. *The Americans as They Are: Described in a Tour Through the Valley of the Mississippi*. London: Hurst, Chance, and Company, 1828.

Stoddard, Amos. *Sketches: Historical and Descriptive, of Louisiana*. Philadelphia: Mathe Carey, 1812.

Whipple, Henry. *Bishop Whipple's Southern Diary, 1843–1844*, edited by Lester Shippee. 1937. Reprint, New York: DaCapo, 1968.

CITY DIRECTORIES

[Campbell's], *The Southern Business Directory and General Commercial Advertiser*. Charleston, S.C.: Walker and James, 1854.

Cohen's New Orleans Directory for 1855. New Orleans: Office of the *Daily Picayune*, 1855.

Cohen's New Orleans and Lafayette Directory . . . for 1851. New Orleans: Office of the *Daily Delta*, 1851.

Gibson's Guide and Directory to the State of Louisiana and the Cities of New Orleans and Lafayette. New Orleans: John Gibson, 1838.

Michel & Co. New-Orleans Annual and Commercial Directory, for 1843. New Orleans: Justin L. Sollée, 1842.

Michel and Co. New Orleans Annual [Directory] and Commercial Register for 1846. New Orleans: E. A. Michel and Company, n.d.

Michel's New Orleans Annual and Commercial Register . . . for 1834. New Orleans: Gaux and Sollée, 1833.

[Michel's] *New Orleans Directory and Register*. New Orleans: J. L. Sollée, 1841.

Mygatt & Co's Directory. 1857.

New-Orleans Directory. 1835.

New Orleans Directory for 1842. New Orleans: Pitts and Clarke, 1842.

[Paxton's] *The New-Orleans Directory and Register*. New Orleans: Benjamin Levy and Company, 1822.

[Paxton's] *The New-Orleans Directory and Register*. New Orleans: Benjamin Levy and Company, 1823.

[Paxton's] *The New-Orleans Directory and Register*. New Orleans: A. T. Penniman and Company, 1830.

[Paxton's] *A Supplement to the New-Orleans Directory of the Last Year*. 1824.

OTHER PRIMARY SOURCES

Abbott, Edith, ed. *Immigration: Select Documents and Case Records*. Chicago: University of Chicago Press, 1924.

Andrews, William L, ed. *From Fugitive Slave to Free Man: The Autobiographies of William Wells Brown*. New York: Mentor, 1993.

Botkin, B. A., ed. *Lay My Burden Down: A Folk History of Slavery*. 1945. Reprint, Athens: University of Georgia Press, 1973.

Brown, William Wells. *Narrative of William Wells Brown*. In *Five Slave Narratives*, edited by William Loren Katz. 1847. Reprint, New York: Arno Press and the *New York Times*, 1969.

Bullard, Henry A. "A Discourse on the Life, Character and Writings of François-Xavier Martin." In *Historical Collections of Louisiana*, edited by B. F. French, 2:17–40. Philadelphia: Daniels and Smith, 1850.

Bullard, Henry A., and Thomas Curry. *A New Digest of the Statutes of the State of Louisiana*, volume 1. New Orleans, 1842.

Chambers, William. *American Slavery and Colour*. 1857. Reprint, New York: Negro Universities Press, 1968.

Conrad, Glenn R. ed. *Land Records of the Attakapas District*, volume 1. Lafayette: University of Southwestern Louisiana, 1990.

Craft, William. *Running a Thousand Miles for Freedom, or the Escape of William and Ellen Craft from Slavery*. 1860. Reprint, Baton Rouge: Louisiana State University Press, 1999.

Douglass, Frederick. *My Bondage and My Freedom*, edited by William L. Andrews. 1855. Reprint, Urbana: University of Illinois Press, 1987.

——. *Narrative of the Life of Frederick Douglass*. 1845. Reprint, New York: Signet, 1968.

Dowler, Bennett. "Tableau of the Yellow Fever of 1853." In *Cohen's New Orleans Directory for 1854*. New Orleans: Office of the *Daily Picayune*, 1854.

——. "Tableaux, Geographical, Commercial, Geological and Sanitary of New Orleans." In *Cohen's New Orleans and Lafayette Directory for 1852*. New Orleans: Office of the *Daily Delta,* 1852.

"The Late Henry Adams Bullard." *DeBow's Review* 12 (January 1852): 50–56.

Jay, William. "Condition of the Free People of Color." In *The Free People of Color*, 371–95. 1838. Reprint, New York: Arno Press and the *New York Times*, 1969.

Kamphoefner, Walter D., et al., eds., *News from the Land of Freedom: German Immigrants Write Home*, translated by Susan Carter Vogel. Ithaca, N.Y.: Cornell University Press, 1988.

Kapp, Friedrich. *Immigration and the Commissioners of Emigration of the State of New York*. 1870. Reprint, New York: Arno, 1969.

"Memoir of Hon. Henry Adams Bullard, LL.D." In *Historical Collections of Louisiana*, volume 3, edited by B. F. French, 5–8. New York: D. Appleton, 1851.

Miller, John F. "A Refutation of the Slander and Falsehood Contained in a Pamphlet, Entitled, Sally Miller." New Orleans, 1845. In *Free Blacks, Slaves and Slaveowners in Civil and Criminal Courts: The Pamphlet Literature*, edited by Paul Finkelman, 123–92. New York: Garland, 1988.

Northup, Solomon. *Twelve Years a Slave*, edited by Sue Eakin and Joseph Logsdon. 1853.

Reprint, Baton Rouge: Louisiana State University Press, 1968.

Olmsted, Frederick Law. *The Cotton Kingdom*. 1861. Reprint, New York: Knopf, 1953.

"Passenger List of the Ship 'Elizabeth' Which Arrived at Philadelphia in 1819." *Pennsylvania Magazine of History and Biography* 25 (1901): 257–60.

Perdue, Charles, Jr., Thomas E. Barden, and Robert K. Phillips, eds., *Weevils in the Wheat: Interviews with Virginia Ex-Slaves*. Charlottesville: University of Virginia Press, 1976.

Ripley, C. Peter, and Jeffrey S. Rossbach, eds. *The British Isles, 1830–1865*. Volume 1 of *The Black Abolitionist Papers*. Chapel Hill: University of North Carolina Press, 1985.

"Sally Miller." New Orleans: Office of the *New Orleans Tropic*, 1845. Copy in the collection of the New York Public Library.

U.S. Census. California. 1850, 1860.

U.S. Census. Louisiana. 1820, 1830, 1840, 1850.

[Whitaker, John Smith]. "Sketches of the Life and Character in Louisiana—The Portraits Selected Principally from the Bench and Bar." New Orleans: Ferguson and Crosby, 1847.

Secondary Sources

BOOKS

Alexander, Elizabeth Urban. *Notorious Woman: The Celebrated Case of Myra Clark Gaines*. Baton Rouge: Louisiana State University Press, 2001.

Anonymous. *Biographical and Historical Memoirs of Louisiana*, volume 1. Chicago: Goodspeed, 1892.

Arthur, Stanley Clisby. *Old New Orleans*. Gretna, La.: Pelican, 1990.

Ayers, Edward L. *Vengeance and Justice: Crime and Punishment in the Nineteenth-Century American South*. New York: Oxford, 1974.

Bailey, John. *The Lost German Slave Girl*. Sydney, Australia: Macmillan, 2003.

Balleisen, Edward J. *Navigating Failure: Bankruptcy and Commercial Society in Antebellum America*. Chapel Hill: University of North Carolina Press, 2001.

Bancroft, Frederic. *Slave Trading in the Old South*. Baltimore: J. H. Furst, 1931.

Bergerie, Maurine. *They Tasted Bayou Water: A Brief History of Iberia Parish*. New Orleans: Pelican, 1962.

Berlin, Ira. *Many Thousands Gone: The First Two Centuries of Slavery in North America*. Cambridge, Mass: Belknap Press of Harvard University Press, 1998.

———. *Slaves Without Masters: The Free Negro in the Antebellum South*. New York: Pantheon, 1974.

Billings, Warren M., ed. *Historic Rules of the Supreme Court of Louisiana, 1813–1879*. Lafayette, La: University of Southwestern Louisiana Press, 1985.

Blassingame, John W. *Black New Orleans, 1860–1880*. Chicago: University of Chicago Press, 1973.

———. *The Slave Community: Plantation Life in the Antebellum South*, revised and enlarged edition. New York: Oxford University Press, 1978.

Bleser, Carol, ed. *Tokens of Affection: Letters of a Planter's Daughter in the Old South*. Athens: University of Georgia Press, 1996.

Brasseaux, Carl A. *The Courthouses of Louisiana*. Lafayette: University of Southwestern Louisiana Press, 1977.

Brasseaux, Carl A., Keith P. Fontenot, and Claude F. Oubre. *Creoles of Color in the Bayou Country*. Jackson: University of Mississippi Press, 1994.

Brody, Jennifer DeVere. *Impossible Purities: Blackness, Femininity, and Victorian Culture*. Durham, N.C.: Duke University Press, 1998.

Broers, Michael. *Europe Under Napoleon, 1799–1815*. London: Arnold, 1996.

Brown, William Wells. *Clotel*. In *Three Classic African-American Novels*, edited by William L. Andrews. 1853. Reprint, New York: Penguin, 1990.

Cable, George Washington. *Strange True Stories of Louisiana*. New York: Scribner's, 1889.

Carrigan, Jo-Ann. *The Saffron Scourge: A History of Yellow Fever in Louisiana, 1791–1905*. Lafayette: University of Southwestern Louisiana Press, 1994.

Carrington, Ulrich. *The Making of an American: An Adaptation of Memorable Tales by Charles Sealsfield*. Dallas: Southern Methodist University Press, 1972.

Castellanos, Henry C. *New Orleans As It Was: Episodes of Louisiana Life*. 1905. Reprint, Baton Rouge: Louisiana State University Press, 1978.

Christovich, Mary Louise, et al. *The American Sector*. Volume 2 of *New Orleans Architecture*. Gretna, La.: Pelican, 1972.

Clark, John G. *New Orleans, 1718–1812: An Economic History*. Baton Rouge: Louisiana State University Press, 1970.

Cleman, John. *George Washington Cable Revisited*. New York: Twayne, 1996.

Cobb, Thomas R. R. *An Inquiry into the Law of Negro Slavery in the United States of America*, volume 2. Philadelphia: T. and J. W. Johnson, 1858.

Conrad, Glenn R., ed. *A Dictionary of Louisiana Biography*. 2 volumes. New Orleans: Louisiana Historical Association, 1988.

Cooper, William J., Jr. *The South and the Politics of Slavery, 1828–1856*. Baton Rouge: Louisiana State University Press, 1978.

Crété, Liliane. *Daily Life in Louisiana, 1815–1830*, translated by Patrick Gregory. Baton Rouge: Louisiana State University Press, 1981.

Dargo, George. *Jefferson's Louisiana: Politics and the Clash of Legal Traditions*. Cambridge, Mass: Harvard University Press, 1975.

Davis, F. James. *Who Is Black? One Nation's Definition*. State College: Pennsylvania State University Press, 1991.

Degler, Carl N. *Neither White nor Black: Slavery and Race Relations in Brazil and the United States*. New York: Macmillan, 1971.

Dominguez, Virginia R. *White by Definition: Social Classification in Creole Louisiana*. New Brunswick, N.J.: Rutgers University Press, 1986.

Duffy, John, ed. *The Rudolph Matas History of Medicine in Louisiana*, 2 volumes. Baton Rouge: Louisiana State University Press, 1958.

Dufour, Charles. *Ten Flags in the Wind: The Story of Louisiana.* New York: Harper and Row, 1967.

Ellis, Geoffrey. *The Napoleonic Empire.* New York: Macmillan, 1991.

Farrison, William E. *William Wells Brown: Author and Reformer.* Chicago: University of Chicago Press, 1969.

Faust, Albert B. *The German Element in the United States.* 1927. Reprint, New York: Arno Press and the *New York Times,* 1969.

Fogleman, Aaron S. *Hopeful Journeys: German Immigration, Settlement, and Political Culture in Colonial America, 1717–1775.* Philadelphia: University of Pennsylvania Press, 1996.

Follett, Richard. *The Sugar Masters: Planters and Slaves in Louisiana's Cane World, 1820–1860.* Baton Rouge: Louisiana State University Press, 2005.

Fortier, Alcée. *The American Domination, 1803–1861.* Volume 3 of *History of Louisiana.* New York, 1904.

Frederickson, George M. *The Black Image in the White Mind: The Debate on Afro-American Character and Destiny, 1817–1914.* New York: Harper and Row, 1971.

———. *White Supremacy: A Comparative Study in American and South African History.* New York: Oxford University Press, 1995.

Garvey, Joan B., and Mary Lou Widmer, *Beautiful Crescent: A History of New Orleans,* 4th edition. New Orleans: Garmer, 1982.

Genovese, Eugene D. *Roll, Jordan, Roll: The World the Slaves Made.* New York: Vintage, 1976.

Goldfield, David. *Cotton Fields and Skyscrapers: Southern City and Region, 1607–1980.* Baton Rouge: Louisiana State University Press, 1982.

Gross, Ariela J. *Double Character: Slavery and Mastery in the Antebellum Southern Courtroom.* Princeton, N.J.: Princeton University Press, 2000.

Guillet, John C., and Robert N. Smith. *Louisiana's Architectural and Archeological Legacies.* Nachitoches, La.: Northwestern State University Press, 1982.

Haizlip, Shirlee Taylor. *The Sweeter the Juice: A Family Memoir in Black and White.* New York: Touchstone, 1994.

Hatcher, William B. *Edward Livingston.* Baton Rouge: Louisiana State University Press, 1940.

Huber, Leonard V. *New Orleans: A Pictorial History.* Gretna, La.: Pelican, 1991.

———. *New Orleans As It Was in 1814–1815.* New Orleans: Battle of New Orleans 150th Anniversary Committee of Louisiana, 1965.

Hunt, Alfred N. *Haiti's Influence on Antebellum America.* Baton Rouge: Louisiana State University Press, 1998.

Hunt, Gaillard. *As We Were: Life in America 1814.* 1914. Reprint, Stockbridge, Mass: Berkshire House, 1993.

Ingersoll, Thomas N. *Mammon and Manon in Early New Orleans: The First Slave Society in the Deep South, 1718–1819.* Knoxville: University of Tennessee Press, 1999.

Jardin, André, and André-Jean Tudesq. *Restoration and Reaction, 1815–1848,* translated by Elborg Forster. New York: Cambridge University Press, 1983.

Johnson, Walter S. *Soul by Soul: Life Inside the Antebellum Slave Market.* Cambridge, Mass: Harvard University Press, 1999.

Jordan, Winthrop D. *White Over Black: American Attitudes Toward the Negro, 1550–1812*. Chapel Hill: University of North Carolina Press, 1968.

Kein, Sybil. *Creole: The History and Legacy of Louisiana's Free People of Color*. Baton Rouge: Louisiana State University Press, 2000.

Kendall, John S. *History of New Orleans*, volume 2. Chicago: Lewis, 1922.

Kilbourne, Richard Holcombe, Jr. *A History of the Louisiana Civil Code, 1803–1839*. Baton Rouge: Louisiana State University Press, 1987.

———. *Louisiana's Commercial Law: The Antebellum Period*. Baton Rouge: Louisiana State University Press, 1980.

King, Grace, and John Ficklen. *A History of Louisiana*, 3d revised edition. New York: University Publishing, 1897.

King, Wilma. *Stolen Childhood: Slave Youth in Nineteenth Century America*. Bloomington: Indiana University Press, 1995.

Kluger, Richard. *Simple Justice*. New York: Knopf, 1975.

Lemann, Bernard. *The Vieux Carré: A General Statement*. New Orleans: Samuel Wilson, Jr., Publications Fund of the Louisiana Landmarks, 1966.

Levine, Bruce. *The Spirit of 1848: German Immigrants, Labor Conflict and the Coming of the Civil War*. Urbana: University of Illinois Press, 1992.

Long, Alecia P. *The Great Southern Babylon: Sex, Race, and Respectability in New Orleans, 1865–1920*. Baton Rouge: Louisiana State University Press, 2004.

Mallinckrodt, Anita M. *From Knights to Pioneers: One German Family in Westphalia and Missouri*. Carbondale: University of Southern Illinois Press, 1994.

Martin, François-Xavier. *The History of Louisiana From the Earliest Period*. 1882. Reprint, New Orleans: Pelican, 1963.

Martin, Jonathan D. *Divided Mastery: Slave Hiring in the American South*. Cambridge, Mass: Harvard University Press, 2004.

Montagu, Ashley. *Man's Most Dangerous Myth: The Fallacy of Race*, revised edition. New York: Harcourt Brace Jovanovich, 1964.

Moody, Alton V. *Slavery on Louisiana Sugar Plantations*. 1924. Reprint, New York: AMS Press, 1976.

Morris, Laura Newell. *Human Populations: Genetic Variation and Evolution*. San Francisco: Chandler, 1971.

Morris, Thomas D. *Southern Slavery and the Law, 1619–1860*. Chapel Hill: University of North Carolina Press, 1996.

Murray, Pauli. *Proud Shoes: The Story of an American Family*. New York: Harper and Row, 1984.

Nadel, Stanley. *Little Germany: Ethnicity, Religion and Class in New York City, 1845–1880*. Urbana: University of Illinois Press, 1990.

Nau, John F. *The German People of New Orleans, 1850–1900*. Leiden: Brill, 1958.

Osborne, Richard H., ed. *The Biological and Social Meaning of Race*. San Francisco: Freeman, 1971.

O'Toole, James. M. *Passing for White: Race, Religion, and the Healy Family, 1820–1920*. Amherst: University of Massachusetts Press, 2002.

Poesch, Jessie, and Barbara Bacot, eds. *Louisiana Buildings, 1720–1940*. Baton Rouge: Louisiana State University Press, 1997.

Raimon, Eve Allegra. *The "Tragic Mulatta" Revisited: Race and Nationalism in Nineteenth-Century Antislavery Fiction*. New Brunswick, N.J.: Rutgers University Press, 2004.

Reinders, Robert C. *The End of an Era: New Orleans in the 1850s*. New Orleans: Pelican, 1964.

Rippley, LaVern J. *The German-Americans*. Boston: Twayne, 1976.

Rothman, Adam. *Slave Country: American Expansion and the Origins of the Deep South*. Cambridge, Mass.: Harvard University Press, 2005.

Rousey, Dennis. *Policing the Southern City: New Orleans, 1805–1889*. Baton Rouge: Louisiana State University Press, 1996.

Rubin, Louis D. *George W. Cable: The Life and Times of a Southern Heretic*. New York: Pegasus, 1969.

Samuel, Martha Ann Brent, and Ray Samuel. *The Great Days of the Garden District and the Old City of Lafayette*. New Orleans: Parents' League of the Louise S. McGehee School, 1961.

Schafer, Judith Kelleher. *Becoming Free, Remaining Free: Manumission and Enslavement in New Orleans, 1846–1852*. Baton Rouge: Louisiana State University Press, 2003.

———. *Slavery, the Civil Law and the Supreme Court of Louisiana*. Baton Rouge: Louisiana State University Press, 1994.

Schultz, Stanley K. *Constructing Urban Culture: American Cities and City Planning, 1800–1920*. Philadelphia: Temple University Press, 1989.

Schwartz, Marie Jenkins. *Born in Bondage: Growing Up Enslaved in the Antebellum South*. Cambridge, Mass: Harvard University Press, 2000.

Searight, Sarah. *New Orleans*. New York: Stein and Day, 1973.

Shugg, Roger. *Origins of Class Struggle in Louisiana: A Social History of White Farmers and Laborers during Slavery and After, 1840–1875*. Baton Rouge: Louisiana State University Press, 1939.

Silverman, Dan P. *Reluctant Union: Alsace-Lorraine and Imperial Germany, 1871–1918*. State College: Pennsylvania State University Press, 1972.

Sinclair, Harold. *The Port of New Orleans*. Garden City, N.Y.: Doubleday and Doran, 1942.

Sitterson, Joseph Carlyle. *Sugar Country: The Cane Sugar Industry in the South, 1753–1950*. Lexington: University Press of Kentucky, 1953.

Somers, Dale A. *The Rise of Sports in New Orleans, 1850–1900*. Baton Rouge: Louisiana State University Press, 1972.

Spickard, Paul, and G. Reginald Daniel, eds. *Racial Thinking in the United States: Uncompleted Independence*. Notre Dame: University of Notre Dame Press, 2004.

Stampp, Kenneth M. *The Peculiar Institution: Slavery in the Ante-Bellum South*. New York: Vintage, 1956.

Starobin, Robert S. *Industrial Slavery in the Old South*. New York: Oxford University Press, 1970.

Starr, Frederick S. *Southern Comfort: The Garden District of New Orleans, 1800–1900*. Cambridge, Mass: MIT Press, 1989.

Stephenson, Wendell Holmes. *Isaac Franklin: Slave Trader and Planter of the Old South*. Baton Rouge: Louisiana State University Press, 1938.

Tadman, Michael. *Speculators and Slaves: Masters, Traders and Slaves in the Old South*. Madison: University of Wisconsin Press, 1989.

Takaki, Ronald. *Iron Cages: Race and Culture in Nineteenth Century America*. New York: Knopf, 1979.

Tallant, Robert. *The Romantic New Orleanians*. New York: Dutton, 1950.

Talty, Stephan. *Mulatto America, at the Crossroads of Black and White Culture: A Social History*. New York: HarperCollins, 2003.

Taylor, Joe Gray. *Negro Slavery in Louisiana*. Baton Rouge: Louisiana State University Press, 1963.

Tenzer, Lawrence R. *The Forgotten Cause of the Civil War: A New Look at the Slavery Issue*. Manahawkin, N.J.: Scholars' Publishing House, 1997.

Toldedano, Roulhac. *The National Trust Guide to New Orleans*. New York: Wiley, 1996.

Tregle, Joseph G., Jr. *Louisiana in the Age of Jackson*. Baton Rouge: Louisiana State University Press, 1999.

Vassberg, Liliane M. *Alsatian Acts of Identity*. Philadelphia: Multilingual Matters, 1993.

Villeré, Sidney Louis. *Jacques Philip Villeré: First Native-Born Governor of Louisiana, 1816–1820*. New Orleans: Historic New Orleans Collection, 1981.

Voss, Louis. *Louisiana's German Heritage: Louis Voss' Introductory History*, edited by Don R. Tolzmann. 1927. Reprint, Bowie, Md.: Heritage Books, 1994.

Wade, Richard C. *Slavery in the Cities: The South, 1820–1860*. New York: Oxford University Press, 1964.

Wahl, Jenny Bourne, *The Bondsman's Burden: An Economic Analysis of the Common Law of Southern Slavery*. New York: Cambridge University Press, 1998.

Walker, Mack. *Germany and the Emigration, 1816–1885*. Cambridge, Mass: Harvard University Press, 1964.

Wall, Bennett H., et al. *Louisiana: A History*, 3d edition. Wheeling, Ill.: Harlan Davidson, 1997.

White, Deborah Gray. *Arn't I a Woman? Female Slaves in the Plantation South*. New York: Norton, 1985.

Wiethoff, William E. *A Peculiar Humanism: The Judicial Advocacy of Slavery in the High Courts of the Old South, 1820–1850*. Athens: University of Georgia Press, 1996.

Williams, Gregory Howard. *Life on the Color Line: The True Story of a White Boy Who Discovered He Was Black*. New York: Dutton, 1995.

Williamson, Joel. *New People: Miscegenation in the United States*. Baton Rouge: Louisiana State University Press, 1995.

Wilson, Carol. *Freedom at Risk: The Kidnapping of Free Blacks in American, 1780–1865*. Lexington: University Press of Kentucky, 1994.

Wokeck, Marianne S. *Trade in Strangers: The Beginnings of Mass Migration to North America*. State College: Pennsylvania State University Press, 1999.

DISSERTATIONS AND THESES

Berchtold, Raimond. "The Decline of German Ethnicity in New Orleans, 1880–1930." M.A. thesis, University of New Orleans, 1984.

Spletstoser, Frederick M. "Back Door to the Land of Plenty: New Orleans As an Immigrant Port," volume 1. Ph.D. diss., Louisiana State University, 1978.

ARTICLES

Baron, John H. "Paul Emile Johns of New Orleans: Tycoon, Musician, and Friend of Chopin." In *Report of the Eleventh Congress* [of the International Musicological Society], 246–50. Copenhagen, 1972.

Barrett, Lindon. "Hand-Writing: Legibility and the White Body in *Running a Thousand Miles for Freedom*." *American Literature* 69 (June 1997): 315–36.

Bonquois, Dora J. "The Career of Henry Adams Bullard, Louisiana Jurist, Legislator, and Educator." *Louisiana Historical Quarterly* 23 (October 1940): 999–1106.

Brasseaux, Carl A. "Entertainment, Sports, and Recreation in New Iberia, 1830–1978." In *New Iberia: Essays on the Town and Its People*, 2d ed., compiled by Glenn R. Conrad, 360–93. Lafayette: University of Southwestern Louisiana, 1986.

———. "French Immigration, 1820–1839." In *The Louisiana Purchase Bicentennial Series in Louisiana History*, edited by Carl A. Brasseaux. Volume 10, *A Refuge for All Ages: Immigration in Louisiana History*, 323–49. Lafayette: University of Southwestern Louisiana Press, 1996.

Bretting, Agnes. "Organizing German Immigration: The Role of State Authorities in Germany and the United States." In *America and the Germans: An Assessment of a 300-Year History*, edited by Frank Trommler and Joseph McVeigh, 1: 25–38. Philadelphia: University of Pennsylvania Press, 1985.

Brown, Steven E. "Sexuality and the Slave Community." *Phylon* 42 (spring 1981): 1–10.

Cable, George Washington. "Salome Müller." *Century Magazine* 38 (May 1889): 56–69.

Clinton, Catherine. "'Southern Dishonor': Flesh, Blood, Race, and Bondage." In *In Joy and in Sorrow: Women, Family, and Marriage in the Victorian South, 1830–1900*, edited by Carol Bleser, 52–68. New York: Oxford University Press, 1991.

Conrad, Glenn R. "Wilderness Paradise: A Glimpse of Jefferson Island and Its Owners for the Past Two Centuries." *Attakapas Gazette* 15 (1979): 52–63.

Dart, Henry Plauché. "The History of the Supreme Court of Louisiana." *Louisiana Historical Quarterly* 4 (1921): 14–71.

Dart, William Kernan. "The Justices of the Supreme Court." *Louisiana Historical Quarterly* 4 (January 1921): 113–24.

Deiler, J. Hanno. "The System of Redemption in the State of Louisiana," translated by Louis Voss. *Louisiana Historical Quarterly* 12 (1929): 426–47.

Donaldson, Gary A. "Bringing Water to the Crescent City: Benjamin Latrobe and the New Orleans Waterworks System." *Louisiana History* 28 (1987): 381–96.

————. "A Window on Slave Culture: Dances at Congo Square in New Orleans, 1800–1862." *Journal of Negro History* 69 (1984): 63–72.

Dufour, Charles. "The People of New Orleans." In *The Past As Prelude: New Orleans, 1798–1968*, edited by Hodding Carter, 2–50. New Orleans: Tulane University, 1968.

Eisterhold, John A. "Lumber and Trade in the Lower Mississippi Valley and New Orleans, 1800–1860." *Louisiana History* 13 (winter 1972): 71–91.

Fernandez, Mark F. "From Chaos to Continuity: Early Reforms of the Supreme Court of Louisiana, 1845–1852." *Louisiana History* 28 (1987): 19–36.

Fischer, Roger A. "Racial Segregation in Antebellum New Orleans." *American Historical Review* 74 (February 1969): 926–37.

Fogleman, Aaron S. "From Slaves, Convicts, and Servants to Free Passengers: The Transformation of Immigration in the Era of the American Revolution." *Journal of American History* 85 (June 1998): 43–76.

Freudenberger, Herman, and Jonathan B. Pritchett, "The Domestic United States Slave Trade: New Evidence." *Journal of Interdisciplinary History* 21 (1991): 447–477.

Gaspard, Elizabeth. "The Rise of the Louisiana Bar: The Early Period, 1813–1839." *Louisiana History* 28 (1987): 183–97.

Gould, Virginia Meacham. " 'If I Can't Have My Rights, I Can Have My Pleasures, and If They Won't Give Me Wages, I Can Take Them.' " In *Discovering the Women in Slavery*, edited by Patricia Morton, 179–201. Athens: University of Georgia Press, 1996.

————. "The House That Was Never a Home: Slave Family and Household Organization, 1820–1850." *Slavery and Abolition* 18 (1997): 90–103.

Gross, Ariela J. "Litigating Whiteness: Trials of Racial Determination in the Nineteenth Century South." *Yale Law Journal* 108 (1998): 109–88.

————. "Reflections on Law, Culture, and Slavery." In *Slavery and the American South*, edited by Winthrop D. Jordan, 57–82. Jackson: University Press of Mississippi, 2003.

Grubb, Farley W. "The Disappearance of Organized Markets for European Immigrant Servants in the United States: Five Popular Explanations Reexamined." *Social Science History* 18 (spring 1994): 1–30.

————. "The End of European Immigrant Servitude in the United States: An Economic Analysis of Market Collapse, 1772–1835." *Journal of Economic History* 54 (December 1994): 794–824.

————. "German Immigration to Pennsylvania, 1709–1820." *Journal of Interdisciplinary History* 20 (winter 1990): 417–36.

————. "Morbidity and Mortality on the North Atlantic Passage: Eighteenth Century German Immigration." *Journal of Interdisciplinary History* 17 (1987): 577–84.

Hardy, James D., Jr. "A Slave Sale in Antebellum New Orleans." *Southern Studies* 23 (fall 1984): 306–14.

Harwood, Thomas F. "The Abolitionist Image of Louisiana and Mississippi." *Louisiana History* 7 (fall 1966): 281–303.

Johnson, Jerah. "New Orleans' Congo Square: An Urban Setting for Early Afro-American Culture Formation." *Louisiana History* 32 (1991): 117–57.

Johnson, Walter S. "The Slave Trader, the White Slave, and the Politics of Racial Determination in the 1850s." *Journal of American History* 87 (June 2000): 13–38.

Jumonville, Florence M. " 'The People's Friend, the Tyrant's Foe': Law-Related New Orleans Imprints, 1803–1860." In *A Law Unto Itself? Essays in the New Louisiana Legal History*, edited by Warren M. Billings and Mark F. Fernandez, 40–57. Baton Rouge: Louisiana State University Press, 2001.

Kendall, John S. "Old New Orleans Houses and Some of the People Who Lived in Them." *Louisiana Historical Quarterly* 20 (1937): 794–820.

———. "Shadow Over the City." *Louisiana Historical Quarterly* 22 (1939): 142–65.

Kotlikoff, Laurence J. "The Structure of Slave Prices in New Orleans, 1804–1862." *Economic Inquiry* 17 (1979): 496–518.

Kotlikoff, Laurence J., and Anton J. Rupert. "Manumission of Slaves in New Orleans, 1827–1846." *Southern Studies* 19 (summer 1980): 172–81.

Logsdon, Joseph. "Immigration through the Port of New Orleans." In *Forgotten Doors: The Other Ports of Entry to the United States*, edited by Mark Stolarik, 105–24. Philadelphia: Balch Institute Press, 1988.

Mitchell, Mary Niall. " 'Rosebloom and Pure White,' or So It Seemed." *American Quarterly* 54 (September 2002): 369–410.

Moltmann, Günter S. "The Migration of German Redemptioners to North America, 1720–1820." In *Colonialism and Migration: Indentured Labor before and after Slavery*, edited by P. C. Emmer, 105–22. Dordrecht: Martinus Nihoff, 1986.

Page, Thomas W. "The Transportation of Immigrants and Reception Arrangements in the Nineteenth Century." *Journal of Political Economy* 19 (1911): 732–49.

Petry, Alice Hall. "The Limits of Truth in Cable's 'Salome Muller.' " *Papers on Language and Literature* 27 (winter 1991): 20–31.

Pritchett, Carla Downer. "Case Law Reporters in Nineteenth Century Louisiana." In *A Law Unto Itself? Essays in the New Louisiana Legal History*, edited by Warren M. Billings and Mark F. Fernandez, 58–75. Baton Rouge: Louisiana State University Press, 2001.

Rankin, David C. "The Tannenbaum Thesis Reconsidered: Slavery and Race Relations in Antebellum Louisiana." *Southern Studies* 18 (spring 1979): 5–31.

Reed, Merl E. "Boom or Bust: Louisiana's Economy During the 1830s." *Louisiana History* 4 (winter 1963): 49–50.

Reinders, Robert C. "Slavery in New Orleans in the Decade Before the Civil War." *Louisiana History* 44 (October 1962): 211–21.

Schafer, Judith Kelleher. "'Guaranteed Against the Vices and Maladies Prescribed by Law': Consumer Protection and the Law of Slave Sales, and the Louisiana Supreme Court, 1809–1862." *American Journal of Legal History* 31 (October 1987): 306–21.

———. "New Orleans Slavery in 1850 As Seen in Advertisements." *Journal of Southern History* 47 (February 1981): 33–56.

————. "Slaves and Crime: New Orleans, 1846–1862." In *Local Matters: Race, Crime and Justice in the Nineteenth Century South,* edited by Christopher Waldrep and Donald G. Neiman, 53–91. Athens: University of Georgia Press, 2001.

Schweninger, Loren. "A Negro Sojourner in Antebellum New Orleans." *Louisiana History* 20 (1979): 306–8.

Shafer, Robert S. "White Persons Held to Racial Slavery in Antebellum Arkansas." *Arkansas Historical Quarterly* 44 (summer 1985): 134–55.

Skeen, C. Edward. "The Year Without a Summer: A Historical View." *Journal of the Early Republic* 1 (spring 1981): 51–67.

Soniat, Meloncy C. "The Faubourgs Forming the Upper Section of the City of New Orleans." *Louisiana Historical Quarterly* 20 (1937): 192–211.

Steckel, Richard H. "Women, Work, and Health Under Plantation Slavery in the United States." In *More Than Chattel: Black Women and Slavery in the Americas,* edited by David Barry Gaspar and Darlene Clark Hine, 43–60. Bloomington: Indiana University Press, 1996.

Tansey, Richard. "Bernard Kendig and the New Orleans Slave Trade." *Louisiana History* 23 (1982): 159–78.

Trussell James, and Richard Steckel. "The Age of Slaves at Menarche and Their First Birth." *Journal of Interdisciplinary History* 8 (winter 1978): 477–506.

Voss, Louis. "Sally Mueller, The German Slave." *Louisiana Historical Quarterly* 12 (1929): 447–60.

Weaver, Herbert. "Foreigners in Antebellum Towns of the Lower South." *Journal of Southern History* 13 (1947): 63–72.

Weeks, Edward T., Sr., and Glenn R. Conrad. "Some Facts and Traditions About New Iberia." In *New Iberia: Essays on the Town and Its People,* 2d edition, compiled by Glenn R. Conrad, 16–46. Lafayette: University of Southwestern Louisiana, 1986.

Wilson, Carol. "Sally Miller, the White Slave." *Louisiana History* 40 (spring 1999): 133–53.

Wilson, Carol, and Calvin D. Wilson. "White Slavery: An American Paradox." *Slavery and Abolition* 19 (April 1998): 1–23.

Winch, Julie. "Philadelphia and the Other Underground Railroad." *Pennsylvania Magazine of History and Biography* 61 (January 1987): 3–25.

Wokeck, Marianne. "Harnessing the Lure of the Best 'Poor Man's Country': The Dynamics of German-Speaking Migration to British North America, 1683–1783." In *"To Make America": European Immigration in the Early Modern Period,* edited by Ida Altman and James Horn, 204–43. Berkeley: University of California Press, 1991.

Zackodnik, Teresa. "Fixing the Color Line: The Mulatto, Southern Courts, and Racial Identity." *American Quarterly* 53 (September 2001): 420–51.

INDEX

ABOUT THE AUTHOR

Carol Wilson is an associate professor of history at Washington College. She is the author of *Freedom at Risk: The Kidnapping of Free Blacks in America, 1780–1865.* She lives in Chestertown, Maryland, with her husband and son.